Turning Your Business Around

Turning Your Business Around

How to spot the warning signs and keep your business healthy

Mark Blayney

How To Books

To Pat, for all her support

Published in 2002 by
How To Books Ltd, 3 Newtec Place,
Magdalen Road, Oxford, OX4 1RE, United Kingdom.
Tel: (01865) 793806.   Fax: (01865) 248780.
email: info@howtobooks.co.uk
http/www.howtobooks.co.uk

First edition 2002

British Library Cataloguing in Publication Data
A catalogue record for this book is available from
the British Library.

Edited by David Kershaw
Cover design by Baseline Arts Ltd, Oxford

Produced for How To Books by Deer Park Productions
Typeset by Anneset, Weston-super-Mare, North Somerset
Printed and bound by Bell & Bain Ltd., Glasgow, Scotland

Note: The material contained in this book is set out in good
faith for general guidance and no liability can be accepted
for loss or expense incurred as a result of relying in particular
circumstances on statements made in the book. The laws and
regulations are complex and liable to change, and readers should
check the current position with the relevant authorities before
making personal arrangements.

Contents

List of illustrations

Preface

This book is intended for the owners/managers of small and medium-sized businesses who may have had little or no formal management training and, worse, no formal training in how to deal with a business that is getting into difficulty. It has been written with two main purposes in mind. To act as a business:

1. *fire extinguisher* for use in a crisis (if you are firefighting at the moment and you need a tool to help put out the flames)

2. *smoke detector* (to help spot the early warning signs of approaching difficulty while there is still time to do something about it).

Business difficulties are widespread throughout the whole UK. During the recession of 1992, company liquidations were running at over 6,000 a quarter. Even during better times significant numbers of businesses still fail: company liquidations were running at about 3,500 per quarter in the mid-1990s and that figure does not include those partnerships and sole traders who also went out of business.

If you are in difficulty, therefore, the first things to realise are:

- you are not alone

- there are specific skills and techniques that can be used to avoid failure

- that other people have been through this and survived – there are ways out, particularly with help!

Note: To avoid unnecessary complexity in the examples given in this book, VAT is ignored in all cases unless specifically stated.

Mark Blayney

Acknowledgements

To the thinkers, such as John Kay and Michael Porter, who have come up with the ideas; to Sir John Harvey-Jones for his permission to use his quotations; to my ex-colleague Bryan Duggan, for condensing much of modern management theory into usable basic principles (such as the ideas underlying the 'formula for success'); and to the many colleagues, bankers and business people I have worked with and learnt from over the years for their help in permitting me to come up with this pragmatic guide. With particular thanks to Eddie Theobald and Neil Barker for their review of the text.

1

Introduction

By far the most common [business mistake], in the UK at least, is not brought about by doing something but by doing nothing.

Sir John Harvey-Jones

THE IMPORTANCE OF BUSINESS SKILLS

While there are always exceptions, most owner-managers are in business because:

- they went into an existing family business or

- they were good at doing something or selling something and they decided, or were forced by circumstances, to go out on their own.

Neither type of owner-manager will generally have had any formal or structured training in how to manage all the different aspects of running a business, or will even have been advised or will have realised that such training might be useful or necessary.

Very few people are skilled in all the things necessary to run a business. It is simply human nature to have a personal preference for, say, the selling of what you 'do' or the doing of it. That is probably why you went into business in the first place and these are, of course, the things that bring the cash into your business.

But when running a business, simply doing the work is not enough. Once you are your own boss, you very quickly find you are your own bookkeeper, sales exec, production manager, secretary, post-clerk, coffee maker and office cleaner, free to set your own hours and to work for whichever 24 hours a day you want to. When you look at the way many owner-managers carry out the necessary business functions, such as planning, doing the accounts, cold calling for new sales or managing people, many of these tasks are often done poorly, if at all. This is because business owners either do not like or feel confident about the job. The problem is that, when times are good these weaknesses may not be critical to the business's survival but, when times get tough, they may prove fatal. A lack of *functional* skills (e.g. in pushing hard for sales, in managing the cash tightly or in cracking down on inefficiencies or slack in the staff) can be what pushes your business into difficulty in the first place. Worse still, if you have had no formal training in all aspects of business management, you will have had no training in what to do in situations of real trading difficulties or crisis.

No one starts out in business to fail but, for various reasons (see Chapter 4), failures do happen. The skills needed to deal with business difficulties are vital because failures are not, generally, inevitable. Most failures happen largely because the business's managers have allowed the situation to deteriorate over time and are then unable to manage through the resulting crisis.

Time and time again, business people who have set up, run and nurtured a successful business, fail to save it when it gets in to difficulty, largely because of weaknesses in their *situational* skills. These are the knowledge or techniques required so that managers can recognise, face up to and address the situation whilst ensuring they protect themselves from potential personal liability. These weaknesses fall into three areas:

A lack of training in the specific skills and knowledge needed

If you have only ever managed a business that has been growing, you are unlikely to have used or to have acquired the situational skills needed to cope with the specific requirements of a crisis. For example, you are unlikely to know how to make redundancies, or manage the bank's concerns or estimate the risks of wrongful trading.

A lack of ability to deal with a crisis

If a business is to grow strongly through new sales, some of its managers must have good sales skills. As a businessperson you will appreciate that this is largely a matter of horses for courses:

* Some people have a natural aptitude for these skills.
* Others can improve their skills with training and through experience.
* Yet others will simply not have the aptitude to develop those skills in the first place.

You may be lucky and find you have a natural aptitude for dealing with a crisis, but don't rely on this!

A refusal to seek help from specialists

When your home is burning down, you call the fire brigade because they have the equipment, the resources and know-how to deal with such a crisis. The same applies in business. You will need expert help.

MANAGERS ARE CRITICAL IN A CRISIS

What really makes the difference in a crisis situation is how you act. You will need to 'make something happen' by either dealing with the problems or by getting help before it is too late. All too often the first real help a failing business receives is from an insolvency practitioner (an 'IP') who has been introduced too late, only to find one of an assortment of management animals has been at work while things have been getting worse.

If you want to survive, you cannot afford to be any of the following.

A goldfish

A goldfish simply doesn't realise there is a problem until it is too late.

An ostrich

An ostrich won't face up to how serious the problems are, preferring instead to believe that everyone else in the industry is doing badly or that, if only the bank would lend another few thousand, all would be well.

A rabbit in the headlights

A rabbit is frozen into inactivity by:

* fear of the inevitability of the impending crash (a self-fulfilling prophesy if ever there was one)

* an inability to face up to doing what needs to be done to save the business, be it cold calling for sales, getting the books up to date or making redundancies

* paralysis through analysis ('should I do this or that or the other, and what if . . .')

* paralysis through advice (unable to take any action before checking it with a solicitor).

A headless chicken

A headless chicken rushes around making lots of noise and scratching at anything that crosses its path, but it is unable to focus on taking the structured actions needed to tackle the real issues.

The management animal you need to be is the *sheepdog*, remaining in control of the situation, identifying the actions required and staying focused on achieving your objectives of herding your business around the obstacles and distractions back to the safe path.

WHAT TO DO IN TIMES OF DIFFICULTY

There is no shame in your business getting into difficulty. All businesses have their ups and downs. What you must do, however, is the following.

1. Spot the signs as early as possible

Business failures are like smouldering fires: the earlier they are detected, the easier they are to deal with because you have more time and resources to devote to dealing with the problem. The longer you delay, the more the fire takes hold, the stronger it burns, the more resources it consumes and the less you have to fight it with.

Use this book as a smoke detector so you can recognise a deteriorating situation as early as possible, the options available to you and how you can formulate and implement a turnaround plan, getting in expert help as early as possible.

2. Face up to the need to deal with the problem

When you face up to the situation you will be able to:

- assess the causes and seriousness of the situation

- understand the options open to you

- plan your strategy; and most importantly of all

- make something happen.

3. Get help

Get in all the help you need.

4. Remain alert

Once the fire is out and you are rebuilding your business, do not forget to use the techniques in this book regularly as a smoke detector to check for the first warning signs of possible future smouldering fires.

The book offers practical help and information in four sections, covering:

(i)   analysing the symptoms and causes of difficulty;

(ii) stabilising your finances;

(iii) setting your strategy; and

(iv) making it happen.

The action required will have to be tailored to the needs of your business. This book will help by giving you the diagnostic tools needed to ensure you take appropriate action for your specific business. It will also assist you in keeping your business healthy in the future by helping you to think strategically, and it suggests techniques you can use so you can take time out regularly to work *on* your business as well as *in* it.

TAKE THE TIME TO DO A BUSINESS HEALTH CHECK

Answer the following questions with either a 'yes' or a 'no'. Put each question into the context of your own business: does this apply to us, yes or no?

*Do we have
a problem
with this?*

1. Is our industry, sector or market going through significant change?　Yes/no

2. Do we have difficulty in saying what is really different about us – what makes people buy from us rather than our competitors?　Yes/no

3. Do we lack a clear vision/strategy (are we missing a map of where we are going)?　Yes/no

4. Are we overconfident (do we have an unrealistic map)?　Yes/no

5. Are we failing to invest enough for the future (e.g. in training our people; in upgrading our processes and in spending on capital equipment, product development, new products and marketing; or in building up financial reserves by leaving sufficient cash in the business or obtaining facilities or investment)?　Yes/no

6. Do we have a management team that is weak
   because it is missing key functional skills (e.g.
   a finance director), personality types (e.g. an
   ideas person) or that has problems due to the
   personalities involved (an autocrat in charge,
   conflict between key staff)?   Yes/no

7. Is the business going through a major change
   (e.g. high growth, a move of premises or a major
   acquisition) that is stretching our management
   and/or financial resources?   Yes/no

8. Are we failing to face up to necessary changes
   (e.g. succession planning, not bringing in external
   management experience where needed)?   Yes/no

9. Have we got weak financial management?   Yes/no

10. Are our turnover and/or profits stagnating/
    weakening/declining?   Yes/no

11. Have we got all our eggs in one customer or
    supplier basket, or in a big project?   Yes/no

12. Is cash tight and pressure from the bank and
    creditors increasing?   Yes/no

13. Are we suffering from some catastrophic event
    (e.g. a fraud, fire or flood)?   Yes/no

How do you feel about any 'yes' answers you gave?
Confident? Frustrated? Worried? Do you think you answered
any questions dishonestly? Do you think you gave too many
'yes' answers? What do you think other people in your business
or your banker's answers would be to these questions about *your*
business?

2

Turnaround

OBTAINING SUPPORT FOR A TURNAROUND

If your business gets into difficulty, there is an increasing amount of support and assistance available to you to help you turn your business around. There are three main sources of support and assistance.

Government policy

Current UK government policy is to promote a culture of entrepreneurism. Entrepreneurism is seen as being key to the development of new businesses and to future wealth creation in an environment of rapid change and innovation. To this end *insolvency legislation* is currently being modified so that rescues of businesses in difficulty are easier.

The banks

Banks' approach to businesses in difficulty has become more sophisticated in recent years for a variety of reasons:

- They are keen to avoid bad publicity, having learnt their lesson from the amount of bad media coverage they received as a result of the volume of receivership appointments that were made during the recession of the early 1990s.

- They are now able to use the skills they acquired at that time when dealing with companies in difficulty.

- They are under pressure from the Bank of England to support businesses.

- Banks are in business too. Banks need live, ongoing customers because new ones are difficult to find and because it makes sense, wherever possible, to help preserve existing customers who are getting into difficulty. The banks have therefore set up specialist units, which are dedicated to getting customers in difficulty back into the 'good' books.

Insolvency practitioners

The insolvency profession (which has always been heavily involved in forms of turnaround work) is currently developing this area of its services. It is attempting to professionalise what is otherwise pretty much a cottage industry of consultants, company doctors and interim managers. For example, the insolvency profession's trade association has recently rechristened itself the Association of Business Recovery Professionals and is in the process of admitting turnaround professionals who are not licensed insolvency practitioners – a move driven by the changes in the banks' attitudes and approaches towards insolvency.

UNDERSTANDING YOUR OPTIONS

If your business is in difficulty, the options (usually in decreasing order of attractiveness) are as follows:

- *Fix the business* so it becomes a successful growing business (even if you do want to sell it – you will get more for it that way).

- *Sell the business*, generally to someone who can fix it, either by coming in to change what it does or how it does it or by absorbing it into something else. As a business in difficulty, you will get less for it.

- *Shut the business down*, disposing of the assets to settle the liabilities.

Here, the 'fixing it' option is referred to as turnaround.

It is important to realise that Insolvency Act 1986 procedures can be used not only for shutting a business down but also in attempts to rescue a business by way of turnaround or sale. The key Insolvency Act procedures are set out in Figure 1. You need to be aware, however, that the survival of a business through an insolvency procedure does not always mean achieving the survival of the company that originally ran the business.

Example
An administrative receiver is appointed to A Ltd. The insolvency practitioner (IP) might have the following options. To:

• Sell the business as a going concern.

• Sell the business to the company's directors and/or shareholders so they can restart the business (a 'phoenix').

• Sell the business on the basis of a deal that has been negotiated and agreed in advance (a 'pre-packaged receivership'). However, the IP will need to be confident such a deal will obtain the best possible commercial return.

In theory, once the administrative receiver has finished realising sufficient assets to repay his or her appointor and the preferential creditors (see Chapter 5), he or she will hand the remaining assets back into the control of the directors. However, in practice, A Ltd is unlikely to survive as the cash generated from the sale of the assets will be used to settle the company's creditors, in strict order of their priority.

THE CONDITIONS NECESSARY FOR A SUCCESSFUL TURNAROUND

To achieve a successful turnaround, the following are usually required:

• *Some form of viable business* Some core business that has the potential for future growth and profitability and around which the business can be rebuilt.

• *Time* Turnarounds are not instantaneous and, if started too late, will either fail or will require protection through an insolvency procedure.

• *Cash* Turnarounds need money. Costs will often be incurred during the initial restructuring phase (e.g. redundancy costs)

	Company voluntary arrangement (CVA)	Administration	Administrative receivership	Liquidation
What is it?	A rescue procedure for saving the company and maximising the creditors' return through the proposal of a potentially binding deal with the creditors	Appointment of an IP by a court to run the company to achieve specified objectives, which can include a CVA, the survival of the company or a sale of its assets	Appointment of an IP by a floating chargeholder to sell the charged assets (i.e. the business) to enable repayment to the lender	Insolvent liquidations are either compulsory when the court orders the winding up of a company (usually on the basis of a creditors' petition) or a creditors' voluntary liquidation where the shareholders vote to wind the company up
Who is in charge?	Directors	IP	IP	IP
Use in rescues	Can be used to propose a creditor standstill to allow an event to occur (e.g. a sale or an investment) or, more commonly, to propose the partial payment of the company's debts over a specified period in full and final settlement	Can be used to obtain immediate protection for a company to allow a CVA to be proposed or for the sale of the business to be achieved	Can be used to sell the business free of creditors and liabilities other than employee liabilities, which transfer to a purchaser (under legislation referred to as 'TUPE')	The IP will cease trading immediately and look to sell the business's assets
Disadvantages	Takes time to put in place, during which a company can be wound up	Expensive to set up	Requires a floating charge to be in place and the charge-holder (normally a bank) to appoint an IP	
Equivalent procedures for sole traders and partnerships	Individual voluntary arrangement (IVA) Partnership voluntary arrangement (PVA).	Can also be granted over a partnership	N/A	Bankruptcy

Fig. 1. Procedures under the Insolvency Act 1986.

and to finance the future regrowth of the business. This money must be found either from within the business ('bootstrapping') or from outside.

* *Vision* A clear goal to which the business is to be directed, to provide both a target and motivation.

* *Management* Management must have not only the will to achieve the turnaround (it's your plan and vision) but also the skills (functional and situational) to make it happen. Alternatively, management must have access to external resources who can provide these skills when required.

* *Stakeholder support* Management cannot achieve a turnaround on their own – they need to take suppliers, customers, staff, bankers, shareholders and others with them.

* *Confidence in the process* The stakeholders need to understand how the management (who will be regarded as having got the stakeholders into this mess) are going to get them out of it. This must entail a structured approach to deal with the problem.

THE PHASES OF A TURNAROUND

Turnarounds have three key phases: crisis management, stabilisation, and regrowth (see Figure 2). As the turnaround moves through these phases, the focus shifts from managing finance to marketing (see Figure 3).

THE TURNAROUND PROCESS

The key stages of any turnaround can be summarised as follows:

1. Recognising the need for a turnaround

The first and, in some ways, most important step towards solving a problem is realising you have one, how urgent it is, what is causing it and then facing up to it.

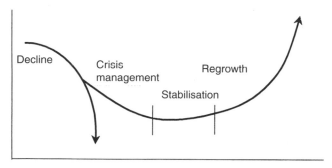

Fig. 2. The phases of a turnaround.

	Crisis management: short-term survival and restructuring down	Stabilisation: preparation for relaunch	Regrowth: Long-term sustainable competitive advantage
Financial	**Concentrate on solving the immediate financial crisis**	Put finance in place for future regrowth	Manage the working capital cycle
People	Retrench staff and keep key staff committed	**Get the right management team in place for regrowth**	Support regrowth by recruiting and retaining the right people
Marketing	Slim down product/market portfolio to profitable items	Prepare for relaunch of growth products	**Drive growth of turnover and profits**

Fig. 3. Priorities in each phase of a turnaround.

2. Surviving in the short term

To survive in the short term you must be able to weather any immediate cash crisis and take a strong grip on your business's finances. You must be alert to what this crisis is telling you about your business's performance and to the reasons for these problems, as well as to possible solutions.

3. Deciding what to do

This involves taking an objective look at what you want to do with your business, as well as at the industry you are in, markets, products, competitive strengths and weaknesses, etc. You then need to come up with a broad picture of the key issues and your proposed strategy and priorities, both long- and short-term.

This information then needs to be used to generate the detailed action plans that will set out who is going to do what, when and with what projected results. Often you will need to do diagnostic work in certain areas, examining your performance to obtain a better understanding of the causes of the under-performance and to identify a possible remedy. You need to prepare marketing plans and forecasts and you need to organise (or perhaps reorganise) your management team so as to achieve the planned milestones, budgets and objectives.

4. Doing it

You must obtain whatever essential support you need from your suppliers, customers, employees and the bank (the 'stake-holders') to ensure the plan can happen and that the required financial resources are in place.

Then manage, manage, manage:

- Manage *the people*: not only yourself and your team but also the stakeholders. Keep them involved and informed as the process unfolds and develops.

- Manage *the process*: identify and capture the value of every 'quick win' so that the plan shows positive results all the way through. Monitor progress and take steps to identify and deal with slippages. Also keep an eye on the plan. Circumstances will change over time and, if they do, your plan has to change. If it does, ensure you communicate this change and the reasons for it to the stakeholders.

- Manage *the business*: keep an eye on the finances and ensure that the process of change does not distract you from the need to continue to manage day-to-day business as well as, if not better than, before.

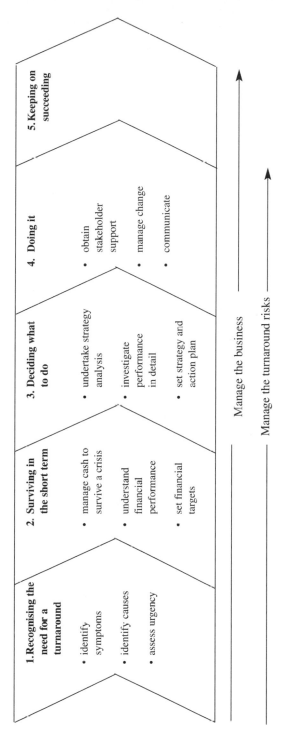

1. Recognising the need for a turnaround

- identify symptoms
- identify causes
- assess urgency

2. Surviving in the short term

- manage cash to survive a crisis
- understand financial performance
- set financial targets

3. Deciding what to do

- undertake strategy analysis
- investigate performance in detail
- set strategy and action plan

4. Doing it

- obtain stakeholder support
- manage change
- communicate

5. Keeping on succeeding

Manage the business

Manage the turnaround risks

Fig. 4. Turnaround management.

- Manage *the turnaround risks*: keep an eye on the risks you may be running whilst operating a business in difficulty, and ensure you cover yourself against potential problems (such as directors' personal liability, under a wrongful trading action, for the company's trading losses).

5. Keeping on succeeding

Once your business is heading back in the right direction, don't stop there. Continue to use the skills and approaches you have applied to returning your business to being a success so it continues to prosper. Keep on using your business's finances to assess performance and keep the strategy and business development plan under regular review.

HOW THIS BOOK IS STRUCTURED

Chapters 3–11 are structured around these key stages of the turnaround process (see Figure 4). The emphasis, however, is firmly on the first two stages because:

- an initial diagnosis of the causes of the difficulty is critical to setting out formal objectives, strategy and action plans; and because

- surviving the initial financial crisis is the critical period that determines whether the business will survive and is also the time when the absence of situational skills and experience is most acute.

3

Spotting the Warning Signs of Business Failure

WHY BUSINESSES FAIL

To understand why businesses fail we need to recognise two complementary truths:

1. *All businesses are fundamentally the same.* All businesses have to buy in and sell on goods and/or services to their customers, who will keep on buying if the offer provides value in satisfying their needs. All businesses must try to make a profit. They also need to manage their employees, sales, production, premises and cash and to collect in their debts, pay their suppliers, submit their tax returns and so on. All businesses therefore need to undertake the same functions.

2. *All businesses are fundamentally different.* Businesses comprise different people operating in different cultures that have different values, expectations and experiences. Businesses do things in different ways, sell different goods and/or services and offer different values to different customers with whom they have different relationships. They all have a unique 'recipe' for what they do and how they do it.

What happens when a business fails, in simple terms, is that it runs out of cash: insolvency is essentially a matter of being unable to pay bills when they fall due. Businesses can run out of cash for a variety of reasons:

- *Lack of profit* – the available cash has been drained away by losses caused by a failure to maintain an appropriate 'recipe'.

- *Excess illiquid assets* – the business has tied up too much of its cash in plant and machinery, property, slow-moving stock, or the development of a new product and thus has insufficient left to fund its trading (see the discussion of the working capital cycle in Chapter 6).

- *Too much growth* – the business's transactions are expanding faster than the cash resources needed to fund them (i.e. it is 'overtrading').

All businesses, therefore, need to manage cash as one of their primary functions. However, problems with either this function and/or the business's recipe will lead to failure in the long term.

THE TYPES OF BUSINESS FAILURE

Business failures generally fall into one of three classic types.

1. The start up that never starts

Statistics show that the majority of businesses cease trading within the first three years. Some of these, however, are not strictly failures but represent the individuals who started up the businesses returning to paid employment. Some of the commonest causes of such failures include the following:

- *The business model is wrong*: the anticipated market does not, in fact, exist.

- The business is *undercapitalised*: it runs out of cash when trying to establish itself and to prove its market.

- The business survives this former stage but hasn't become sufficiently established with enough reserves; it *fails to*

weather a downturn a longer-established business would
survive.

- The business has been set up in a high-growth industry but
  fails to survive the 'shake out'. This is a particularly common
  phenomenon in new or suddenly fashionable sectors (e.g.
  skateboard shops in the 1970s). In such situations many new
  players enter an expanding market to cash in on the
  perceived easy profits, only to find that the sector's initial
  growth slows or even reverses, leaving the rush of entrants
  with overcapacity and facing a slowing or falling demand.
  How many mobile phone shops are there on your high street
  today? How many do you think there will be in five years'
  time?

- *The businessperson has the wrong personality type or lacks
  the determination to see the business through.* For example,
  he or she is is unable or unwilling to face up to necessary
  business tasks, such as cold calling for sales.

2. The catastrophic failure

These types of business failure are surprisingly rare. Such
failures are where the business fails to survive some sort of
traumatic event, such as those listed below. The effects of each
type of event can, in most cases, be significantly reduced by
good management:

- A *major fire* or *flood* may be regarded as an uncontrollable
  'act of God', but businesses should take some steps to plan
  for such eventualities by way of insurance cover and sensible
  contingency planning.

- *Major fraud* can be catastrophic. Therefore the management
  of any business should take responsibility for setting up
  controls to ensure this does not happen. Many frauds start in
  a small way and grow hugely over time, but they can be
  detected by the application of simple controls and
  procedures.

- Occasionally a *governmental Act* can be catastrophic since
  legislative changes can prevent businesses from operating

almost overnight (e.g. legislation to control gun clubs). More often, however, legislation changes the rules by which businesses have to operate. For example, in the 1990s the UK government changed the rules about payments made by local authorities for nursing home services. While such changes can be quite swift, the nature of the political process usually allows some warning. It is also true to say that, in the example just given, not all nursing homes were forced out of business and that it was the good-quality, well managed and well run nursing homes that were best positioned to survive the changes in legislation.

- *Major litigation*, for example, over an alleged patent infringement, can also sink a company. However, it is up to management to have the foresight to deal with this sort of commercial risk.

3. Incremental failure over time

Incremental failure over time is the 'normal' type of failure for an established business.

NORMAL BUSINESS FAILURE

Normal business failure follows what is known as a 'decline curve' and is the result of an accelerating process rather than an individual catastrophic event (Figure 5).

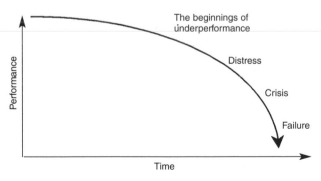

Fig. 5. Normal business failure: the decline curve.

The process starts with simple underperformance that results in poor profitability. Over time, continued underperformance translates into reduced reserves and investment, and the balance sheet starts to show signs of distress. Time and available resources start to run out.

As the business begins to get into real difficulties the slope into crisis becomes steeper. The problems now start to compound each with the other. For example, you are on stop with your supplier so you can't get the raw materials that would allow you to complete an order and so bill your client, but you cannot collect cash from your client until you have completed the whole order. At the same time, interest charges, purchasing inefficiencies and late payment penalties increase costs and eat into your available cash.

Allowing a business to reach this stage must be seen as evidence of weak management. Trying to manage a business in this state is obviously an unpleasant and increasingly difficult task, so no one wants to be in this situation if he or she does not have to be and certainly for no longer than is absolutely necessary. The fact you are in these circumstances indicates you are going to need some kind of outside help in order to change the direction of the curve and to save your business.

If the direction of the curve is not reversed, the business will eventually fail.

AVOIDING FAILURE

In general this book assumes that your business has got past its first three years and is suffering from a 'normal' type of decline. However, having said that, most of the advice in this book is also applicable to potential start-up and catastrophic failures.

To come up with a plan to address the risk of normal failure you need to take the following steps:

1. recognise the symptoms of normal failure;
2. check your business's health to detect the warning signs;
3. recognise the causes of normal failure; and
4. judge how serious things are.

THE SYMPTOMS OF NORMAL FAILURE

As a business slides down the decline curve, the symptoms of decline become more and more apparent in its accounts. The problems with accounts are, however, first, they are, by definition, *backwards looking* and are, therefore, always somewhat out of date (for example, if a company is only producing statutory accounts for filing, this information can be the best part of two years old by the time it has to be made public); and, secondly, there's *none so blind as those who will not see.* Where the results are bad and/or there is weak financial reporting, accounts can be very out of date if people do not want to face up to seeing the reality, or let others (such as the bank) see the actual position. A deteriorating bank balance is bad enough but when this is combined with a delay in producing your accounts, the warning sirens really start to go off in your bank manager's office!

However the signs can also readily be seen in non-financial indicators, and an overall guide to these symptoms is set out below. Unfortunately, this is one of those cases where the more uncomfortable reading this makes, the more you need help.

Underperformance

Underperformance means that:

- your market share and reputation are being lost;
- your turnover is stagnant or reducing;
- your profits are stagnant or declining and, sooner or later, the first losses are being reported; and
- the bank is taking security for its lending (if it doesn't already have it) and is starting to demand more information from you.

Distress

When your business is in distress, the following situations may arise. First, you may find your staff turnover is rising and that your business needs to borrow heavily to fund trading (as a result of its reduced profits). Increased borrowing can lead to the following:

- Your bank overdraft rises. The bank sees a growing 'hardcore' of overdraft debt: your account fails to 'swing' into credit.

- You start to stretch creditor payment terms as you start to rely on more and more creditor funding. This results in higher 'creditor days' and the aged creditor reports begin to show significant older values.

- You are forced to acquire assets on lease or hire purchase you would once have bought outright.

- Despite your dislike of it (because 'it's only something businesses in difficulty do'), you start to think about moving to factoring as a way of getting more lending against your debtors than your bank is giving you.

Secondly, you start to make regular or more severe losses until losses become the norm. You seem to have forgotten you are in business to make a profit and you consider breaking even to be 'good news'. Your credit rating starts to fall as your reported financial performance worsens, and your accounts start to appear later and later. Your audit report is qualified. Next, your relationship with your bank becomes strained, as they start to require regular meetings, more information and projections, further personal guarantees and/or the introduction of an investigating accountant.

Finally, you gamble. You put a disproportionate effort into long-shot big projects that will save your business if they come off rather than facing up to the real here-and-now unpleasant actions you really need to take.

Crisis

When your business is in crisis, your finance director jumps ship or goes off on long-term sickness. Your overdraft is at or over the limit and your bank is bouncing cheques (or threatening to do so) and pressing for a reduction in its exposure. You are making 'payments on account' and/or are actively delaying payments to creditors in an attempt to manage the cash or to stave off failure. Suppliers are demanding payments to clear or reduce their accounts and are placing you on stop. Your statutory payments (PAYE, VAT) are in arrears.

Legal action begins, starting with writs, county court judgements, statutory demands for payment and threats of petitions for winding up your business. The legal pressure increases, with the Inland Revenue and/or HM Customs & Excise sending in bailiffs to take walking possession over your assets. Winding-up petitions are presented. Letters from insolvency practitioners (IPs) and 'debt counsellors' arrive, asking if they can help. IPs eager for a job notify your bank you are in trouble, basing their judgement on the legal actions that are being taken against you (which becomes a self-fulfilling prophesy). Your landlord distrains for unpaid rent.

The next step is failure and insolvency.

CHECKING YOUR BUSINESS'S HEALTH TO SPOT THE WARNING SIGNS

In a real crisis the fire alarm should be sounding good and loud but, if things haven't got to this stage, there are a number of tools and techniques you can use on a regular basis to help you judge whether you have a current or impending problem. These fall into two categories.

Subjective judgements and objective measures

Subjective judgements
Subjective judgements are, in the main, non-financial. They include such measures as the following:

- Assessing whether your business is suffering from any of the symptoms of normal failure as outlined above.

- Using the health check set out at the end of Chapter 1 or an A score test (see the end of this chapter), which will also help you to look at the causes of your problems.

- Seeking an external opinion from such sources as your accountant or bank manager.

Objective measures
Objective measures of a business's financial performance are
based on statistical analyses, such as commercial credit rating
information and 'Z' and 'H' scores.

Surprisingly, perhaps, subjective judgements often give a
better long-term preventative warning of problems since they
look at the forces that will eventually start to show through in
poor financial results. Financially based measures, on the other
hand, pick up on poor or declining performance that must
already be showing up clearly in the trading figures and, for
companies in difficulties, this sort of information can be
seriously out of date.

To obtain most value from subjective tests, you should not
only perform them yourself but should also use them to obtain
others' views. Get your managers to do them as well (preferably
on an anonymous basis so you obtain an honest view) so that
you can test your findings against theirs. Find an external
adviser whom you trust and ask him or her to provide you with
his or her views as well. This helps to avoid 'group think' where
members of the management team (who are all sharing the same
bunker) are unhealthily mirroring one particular view of the
situation back to each other.

Identifying the causes of what is going wrong is the first step
to fixing it.

Health check against symptoms and causes

Using the checklist given in Figure 6, tick all those symptoms of
normal failure your company is displaying:

* Which categories do the ticked items fall into:
  underperformance, distress or crisis? Use your results to
  assess how far you have progressed down the decline curve.

* What areas of weakness has this exercise identified?

Once you have completed this exercise, it is worth asking
yourself a further supplementary question: how surprising are
your findings? If they do come as a surprise, why has this
happened? Are you working *in* your business too much, rather
than *on* it? If they do not come as a surprise, the exercise has

simply told you things you already knew. If this is the case, are these things you:

- Are addressing actively?

- Had not thought to be serious?

- Have been avoiding or not facing up to?

Underperformance
Your market share and reputation are being lost
Your turnover is stagnant or reducing
Your profits are stagnant or declining
You are reporting your first losses
The bank is taking security for its lending and is starting to demand
  information

Distress
Staff turnover is rising
You need to borrow more heavily to fund trading
Your bank overdraft is rising
You are starting to make regular or more severe losses
Your credit rating is starting to fall
Your accounts start to appear later and later
Your audit report is qualified
Your relationship with your bank is becoming strained
You are gambling on long-shot big projects rather than facing up to
  the here and now

Crisis
Your finance director leaves
Your overdraft is at or over the limit
You are making 'payments on account' and/or are actively delaying
  payments
Suppliers are demanding payments and are placing you on stop
Your statutory payments are in arrears
Legal actions against you are being started
Legal pressures are increasing
Letters from IPs and 'debt counsellors' arrive
IPs eager for a job notify your bank you are in trouble
Your landlord distrains for unpaid rent

Fig. 6. The symptoms of normal failure.

Accountant/bank manager feedback

You work in one business but your accountant and your bank manager between them deal with hundreds of businesses. As we have seen, whilst all these businesses will be different they will all have the same functions and each will have developed a recipe that works with its type of industry, its clients, its products, staff and owners.

If you seek out and listen to advice accountants and bank managers are able to give you, you will be tapping into a wealth of experience these people have gained through working with businesses that have been confronted with problems similar to your own. Do not, therefore, underestimate the long-term value of good professional advice. In addition, these people may be able to provide you with specific 'benchmarking information' that allows you to compare your performance across a variety of measures and against others in the same industry.

Remember also that your bank has access to what is usually a very telling indication of business health, and that is your bank account.

Example
Figure 7 shows Company B's monthly maximum credit and overdrawn account balances in each month over the last two years. Now you might think a business that has been operating within its facility every month except the last (when it was marginally over) would be one the bank is quite relaxed about. However, even before the accounts for the last two years were published, the bank manager will be worried:

- The account's 'swing' (the movement between its highest and lowest balance in a month) has narrowed dramatically as the company has struggled to keep within its overdraft limit by only issuing cheques against money as it comes in.

- The account is, however, no longer 'swinging' into credit.

- The account's 'headroom' (the unused facility available) has been steadily decreasing and it is now recording its first 'excess' (the balance is over its agreed facility).

- A 'hardcore' of overdraft has been steadily building that

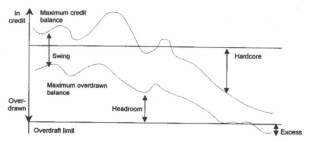

Fig. 7. Company B: maximum and minimum account balances.

is no longer cleared on a regular basis by the account swinging into credit.

In the absence of any other explanation, the bank manager's assumption in these circumstances is that Company B's hardcore overdraft represents the cash effects of sustained trading losses.

Plot this graph for your business. What does it suggest to you?

Please note that where banks prepare this sort of graph, they do so to measure their exposure to you. Their version will therefore have an inverted scale showing exposure climbing as the overdraft grows.

Credit scores

Credit-rating agencies earn some of their income through checking on the health of businesses so as to be able to advise other businesses on the levels of credit to extend. Widely available from a number of sources, these assessments will show you how independent external agencies have assessed your business's financial health on the basis of your published accounts (e.g. some are on the basis of a score from 1–100). They can also be used to provide a snapshot of current, apparent financial health as well as of annual trends.

Z and H scores

Z scores are statistical analyses of business failures that look back at statistics over periods of decades. Such analyses have resulted in the identification of a mix of different financial ratios that are characteristic indicators of failing businesses in various sectors. H scores calculate the same mix of ratios for your own business, compare these to the set for failed businesses and then produce a 'health score' based on how close to, or far from, this group your scores are. This health score is used as a statistical indicator of likely distress (and, by implication, failure) over the next three years.

TAKE AN 'A' SCORE TEST

An A score test uses non-financial signs in a structured way. It makes the assumption that business difficulties stem from problems with management organisation, controls, or the ability to change which, over time, lead to mistakes being made that in turn, lead to real signs and symptoms of difficulty.

To undertake this test, simply look through the statements set out below. If you disagree with a statement, cross out the relevant score; if you agree with it, leave the score as it is. Make each a positive 'yes' or 'no' decision: there are no part marks!

Management	
The business is run by an autocrat	8
The chief executive and chairperson are the same individual	4
The other directors are non-existent, passive or non-contributing	2
Your business lacks directors with all-round skills	2
There is a specific lack of a strong finance director	2
Your business lacks management depth below board level	1
Accounting controls	
There are no budgetary control, budgets or variance reports	3
There are no up-to-date cashflow plans and no or poor knowledge of borrowing requirements	3
Your business has no costing system so that managers do not have accurate information about costs/contributions	3

Ability to change
There is a failure to notice/respond to change in the
business environment (signs include old-fashioned
products, an antiquated factory, ageing directors or no
computers)   15
                                                              ___
                                                               43
Specific risks
The business has relatively high levels of borrowings   15
The company is overtrading (the company is expanding
faster than its funding)   15
The company is exposed to a big project (where the
company is at risk of collapse if failure occurs)   15
                                                              ___
                                                               45
Warning signs
There are real signs of financial difficulty (poor
accounting ratios for sector, poor credit rating)   4
Your business employs creative accounting to
disguise the difficulties   4
There are non-financial signs of difficulty (capital
expenditure decisions delayed, staff turnover rising,
offices in need of repair/renovation)   3
There are terminal signs (the bank is reducing its
overdraft facility, creditor pressure)   1
                                                              ___
                                                               12
                                                              ___
Total possible score   100

Working out your score:

Score	Result
Less than 10	There is unlikely to be any cause for alarm, but why not redo the test in six months' time?
10–25	Some cause for concern. What issues has the test highlighted for you? What actions does this suggest you should consider taking?
Over 25	A serious cause for concern.

4

Understanding Why Businesses Fail

THE CAUSES OF NORMAL FAILURE

The symptoms outlined in the previous chapter are the outward signs of decline. While it is the symptoms that kill you, the real cause of death is the underlying disease.

An unpalatable truth about business failures is that the insolvency practitioners who deal with failures generally think that, if your business has survived its first three years, the most important underlying cause of failure (whatever the precipitating event) will be how you manage your business.

However, on a more positive note, if this is true, you control how you manage your business and so it is totally within your power to do what is needed to save it.

When looking at the causes of failure there are four important points to bear in mind.

1. The situation may appear highly complex

You may find the situation appears highly complex because there will often be a number of levels of causes underlying the business's difficulties. Usually, some primary underlying cause (such as a lack of leadership and/or investment) has allowed a variety of secondary causes (such as inefficient production or a lack of new products) to grow over time until a crisis is precipitated by some specific new cause (such as a new competitor entering the market who uses new technology). This then impacts on a wide variety of areas across the business, leading to many different symptoms, all of which need to be addressed.

One of the ways an experienced outsider can often help in these situations is by providing a fresh pair of eyes to help you to cut through the apparent complexity so as to identify the real issues. In fact, the fundamental issues usually turn out to be the reasons for your inability to address the many individual apparent problems. For example, a lack of leadership might simply arise where a managing director who is shy has inherited a business he did not actually want to run.

2. Short-term requirements must be balanced against long-term requirements

One of the fundamental tricks in running a successful business is to be able continuously to balance short-term requirements with long-term requirements. The short-term requirement is that you need to be generating cash and profits. The long-term requirement is that you need continuously to be reinvesting cash and profits into the future of the business to ensure you satisfy customers (and, hence generate profits and cash) into the future.

With a turnaround, the short-term cash position is likely to be very tight, while refocusing and reviving the business will usually require a long-term reinvestment of time and money. So in a period of turnaround the apparent conflict between these two imperatives will be at its greatest.

3. The whole business needs moving forward simultaneously

As well as balancing the present needs of the business with those of the future, you need to balance the pace of development and change across the different areas of the business so that the whole business moves forward simultaneously, and across all functional areas.

Example
Company C employs 50 people and is looking to double its turnover over three years. As sales expand it has to expand the fulfilment side of its business (i.e. production and delivery) and also the financing of its operations so as to avoid overtrading. This means it must expand its back-office administration to cope with the extra paperwork involved, and its accounting systems will need upgrading to handle the increased functions. It will thus need bigger premises and more staff. As more staff are

recruited and trained so that staffing levels approach 100, the business decides to expand its management team to include a dedicated personnel manager who will look after this function of the business.

If the company's sales had increased but it had not expanded its other supporting functions and resources at the same time, eventually the company would get into difficulties in supplying its customers and might well run out of cash.

4. The approach should be consistent across all areas of the business

You should generally aim to have a consistent approach to your recipe across all areas of your business. If you are looking to deliver a high-quality service to your clients, you will more than likely need high-quality staff who are well trained and who have good backup support systems. If you want to deliver a cheap and cheerful service, you are unlikely to want or need a prestigious office block from which to operate.

THE FIVE KEY AREAS

The causes behind normal business failure can be broken down into five key areas:

1. The business's management structure.

2. The strategy challenges (the big problems that must be managed).

3. Lack of financial control.

4. Lack of operational control.

5. One-off projects or special circumstances that place a heavy demand on the business's resources.

All these circumstances (except, perhaps, for strategy challenges) arise purely as a result of internal factors that are completely within your control. And while strategy challenges generally come from external factors (such as the economy, technical developments or changes in the industry you are in), how your business reacts to and deals with these challenges is entirely up to you.

The remainder of this chapter goes on to look at each of these reasons for normal business failure in turn.

Management structure

The following are but a few of the problems the management structure of a business might inflict upon its performance.

The managing director is an autocrat. While strong leadership is vital to give a business a clear sense of drive and direction, when such leadership is driving a business over a cliff, this type is fatal. Autocrats drive away others with independent views as they see them as challenges to their authority. Autocrats can prevent any form of constructive debate about the best way forward or about what changes need making.

If autocrats have a so-called 'team' around them, these will comprise either loyal drones, 'yes' men, or both. A managing director who leads a team where each person has something meaningful to contribute to the business and whose role is recognised, will be far stronger for it. Conversely, a lack of leadership will create the opposite problems. Where the managing director is weak, no one will be quite sure who is really in charge.

A lack of management experience and depth is a problem typical of 'boards' where membership is limited to people with experience of their own functional areas only (typically sales or production). In such cases the board takes the view that other skills are incidental to the business's success ('after all we have managed without them so far'), and is unwilling to incur the expense of hiring these skills in as managers or to dilute the board's equity by recruiting appropriate new board members.

Where there is a skills problem at board level, there are likely to be more severe problems at the next level down. Such boards are also unwilling to seek or to take external advice, and are certainly reluctant to pay for it. They may also fail to change the management structure/culture (i.e. to manage change), particularly as the business changes in size. How big a business do you think you can sensibly control as a lone entrepreneur? One employee? Ten employees? A hundred? As businesses grow, they need to change the way they work and are controlled by bringing in professional management or directors and, generally, by moving from an entrepreneurial power structure/culture to a functional one. The structure and culture of a business must work together (see Chapter 10). The entrepreneur, therefore, has to decide whether to stay small or to face up to delegating control to others (and the entrepreneur must manage the process of changing to working in this way in a successful manner).

Managements may similarly fail to plan for succession and to allow for generational changes to happen. In 50 years' time, will the survivors of today's thirty-somethings e-business start-ups still be headed by those now eighty-somethings? If not, why not? Where there are major disputes between the owners or managers of a business (or both), effective business management will go to the wall. Managements that fail to face up to problems and to take necessary action in the unrealistic or unjustifiable hope or belief that things will simply get better are putting their faith in the non-existent 'turnaround fairy'.

The view that there is 'nothing we can do' as 'everyone in the whole industry is in difficulties' will be dispelled by an afternoon doing credit searches or by looking at the accounts of a half a dozen competitors. In any industry in difficult there are going to be survivors and failures; the trick is to be in the right category.

Family businesses run in the interests of family members and not the business will likewise suffer as will businesses who fail to focus on running the business for a profit. Businesses need to be run on a commercial basis with an eye on cash and with a constant review of performance, opportunities and costs so that margins (and hence profits) and, ultimately, cash are maximised (i.e. to produce reserves of profit to be ploughed back into the growth and development of the business for the future). Some businesses are run by people *in* business rather than *business people*.

The *bluebottle syndrome* occurs where management actually thrives on, or is unable to manage in any other way than, total

The managing director is an autocrat
Lack of leadership
Lack of management experience and depth
Unwillingness to seek/take external advice
Failure to change the management structure/culture or to manage change
Failure to plan for succession
Shareholder/board disputes
Failure to face up to problems and to take necessary action
Family business run in the interests of family members
Failure to focus on profit
The bluebottle syndrome
The goldfish syndrome
The ostrich syndrome

Fig. 8. Management structure problems.

chaos. The *goldfish syndrome* means failing to understand exactly where you are and where you are going (e.g. the last financial information is the accounts filed two years ago). The *ostrich syndrome* means failing to face up to known problems with either operations or the business recipe. (See Figure 8 for a summary of these problems.)

Strategy challenges

There are many large, often externally created challenges that present threats as well as opportunities to businesses and their recipes, such as significant changes in the nature of an industry which, if not dealt with by updating the recipe to ensure sustained competitive advantage (see Chapter 8), will result in long-term failure.

The first is a failure to spot and adapt to changes in the sector/market's needs. The business recipe may be very successful at the moment but a quick look at what happened to Marks & Spencer will show what happens when a business fails to adjust its recipe to move with the times. Similarly, products or businesses reach the end of their natural lifecycles. Goods and services are introduced as something new, are accepted as the norm and then fade away to be replaced by the new. The timespans of some of these lifecycles can be extremely short (e.g. in fashion and electronic products) due to the increasing rate of change and speed of innovation in a particular sector.

You should continuously review your products and services to ensure you are not left behind and so that you can either 'reinvent' your offering or replace it with the next 'big thing'.

Businesses might also fail to prepare themselves for changes in trade cycles. Over time, an economy must be expected to go through periods of growth and recession. Businesses have to prepare for these cycles and to set their strategy accordingly. (As a recession looms, do you decide to build up your cash reserves or do you go ahead with launching that high-cost luxury version of your product?)

In most cases the best way to manage change and development is to make them an integral part of your business recipe. Changes will happen with minimal disruption as long as the changes are generally all heading in the same direction. In this way you will minimise the risks of change to your business. But there will be some occasions (e.g. when you have fallen badly behind for some reason) where incremental change is not enough and you will have to face up to making major changes.

A high cost structure means it is costing you more to make something than it does your competitors. This can be the result of differences in scale. For example, if you are building 100 cars a year, your costs per car are going to be higher than Toyota, who enjoys 'economies of scale'. Firstly, Toyota's volume means it can buy parts more cheaply than you can. Secondly, Toyota's managing director's salary, advertising budget and all its overheads are being absorbed across millions of cars per year, whilst yours are only spread over 100. Thirdly, in building millions of cars Toyota has gone further down the learning curve of how to make cars efficiently.

Alternatively, a high cost structure might arise as a result of fundamental structural factors. For example, if you are based in the southeast of England you will be paying higher wages and rents than a competitor based in the northeast of England where wages and rents will be lower. Either way, being uncompetitive on costs is usually a recipe for failure – unless you can persuade customers to buy, irrespective of the costs to them.

A lack of investment for the future (in new products,

marketing, staff training, plant and equipment or new technology) is a particular problem for 'lifestyle' businesses designed to support an individual business person's chosen lifestyle which fail to realise they need to reinvest in developing the business's skills, products and contacts to ensure its long-term survival. Alternatively, when you are developing a new part of the business, do not forget to manage the old part. After all, the old part is probably producing the cash needed to fund the new project, and you need to ensure that cash keeps flowing.

The 'eggs in one basket' risk arises from overexposure to circumstances where failure will bring down the whole business. The first type of such risk is the 'bet the company' situation where one big project, one new business line, one acquisition or one contract has been taken on. Before entering into such projects, always look carefully at what the real costs and cashflows are going to be and take a long hard look at the skills you will need to pull the deal off. It is better not to do it than to get halfway through and find you cannot complete it.

Secondly, there are situations where a business is totally reliant on a single product, supplier or customer and its fate, therefore, is not in its own hands (e.g. 50% of sales are to or through one customer or distributor). In these cases, the message is 'diversify or die'. A similar problem is a lack of power in relationships, where over-reliance on a single supplier or customer means they, not you, determine the prices and terms of trade.

Some businesses operate in difficult industries, and different industries have different characteristics which affect how difficult they are to operate in (see Chapter 8). Particular problems arise in industries with any of the following characteristics:

- High exposure to risks that are outside the business's control except by expensive or complex hedging mechanisms (e.g. fluctuating commodity prices or foreign exchange risks).

- Declining markets, particularly in industries that require large investments in plant and equipment or where the costs of exiting the business are high. Ruinous competition can set in as a consequence of a large, fixed capacity chasing smaller and smaller demand.

* A reliance on commodity products, as prices for commodities are set by the markets (unless you can differentiate your product as a brand people will buy for reasons other than price).

The final type of strategy challenge arises as a result of a lack of bank, supplier, customer and staff support. (See Figure 9 for a summary of these challenges.)

Failure to spot and adapt to changes in the sector/market's needs
End of a business's natural lifecycle
Failure to prepare for trade cycles
Failure to face up to the need for step changes
High cost structure
Lack of investment for the future
Concentration on the new to the detriment of the old
Eggs in one basket
Lack of power in relationships
Operating in a difficult industry
Lack of bank/supplier/customer/staff support

Fig. 9. Strategy challenges.

Lack of financial control

Financial control problems fall into three main areas.

Information

To run a business and make sensible business decisions, you need financial information that is timely, meaningful and accurate. If you don't have this you are just guessing at how you are doing or at how much your products really cost to make. You need timely, meaningful and accurate information if you are going to make crucial decisions about how to start to save your business, such as which products or markets to focus on because these are the most profitable ones.

Control

If you don't want to suffer catastrophic failure through fraud, you must put in place adequate financial controls.

Management

You need to manage your business's money, finance and financial strategy. Not doing so often leads to problems with the following:

- *Poor credit control* Producing and selling your goods is only part of the story. Plenty of people will buy your goods if they don't have to pay for them. Getting the money in after the sale is a vital function, as is making sure you do *not* sell to people who cannot, or will not, pay.

- *High stock levels* Holding stock costs money (see Chapter 7).

- *Inappropriate funding* You wouldn't use your personal overdraft (repayable on demand) to buy a house you are going to live in for a long time. Why, then, should you expect your business to fund its long-term assets on an overdraft?

- *Overgearing* If you borrow too heavily you become overexposed as those interest and capital payments have to be made month after month, whatever the trading results.

- *Overtrading* If you grow faster than your supply of funds, your cash will run out.

Lack of operational control

All the day-to-day functions of the business must work and must work correctly if the business is to succeed.

Inefficient production can arise from a variety of causes:

- Is the factory poorly laid out?

- Is the equipment obsolete or poorly maintained?

- Are the workers poorly trained or undermotivated?

- Is production organised in the most appropriate way (single/batch/continuous)?

- Does the business manufacture too wide a range of products?

Quality is a factor in any sale. You may buy a box of matches based on their price, but if you find half the matches don't light you are unlikely to buy another box from the same manufacturer. You must also have an effective salesforce who can get out and sell to customers, as well as an effective distribution system to deliver the goods.

Some businesses also fail to manage 'soft' staff issues. For example, despite his qualifications and experience, is that bright, ambitious ideas man with a mind like a grasshopper and salesman's bow tie, who responds well to praise, really suited to his job in process quality control, managing details day in, day out by the book? If not, why not? To overcome such problems you need to ask yourself the following questions:

- How are you organised? Who does, and reports, what and to whom? Draw an organisation chart for your business with brief job titles. How clear and logical is this chart?

- What are your organisation's culture and structure (see Chapter 10)? Are they appropriate?

- What reward structures do you have in place to encourage specific behaviours (e.g. commission for sales staff)?

- Do you understand what motivates your workers? Are all your staff driven by the same things (praise, security, power, excitement) or do they vary in their needs?

- Do your staff tend naturally to fill different roles in a team (the new ideas person, the boss, the project manager or the tidier-up of loose ends)? Are you using your staff to your best advantage?

- Do your staff have particular characteristics that would suit them better in different jobs? Do these personality issues lead to conflicts (e.g. the salesperson who hates paperwork and who drives production up the wall because of his or her failure to record and specify properly what the customer wants)? What are you doing to manage these sorts of issues?

- What is your natural management style? Direct (a spade is a spade, be it good or bad), influencing (lots of praise for good behaviour, coaching for bad), formal and by the book, with lots of written memos, etc.? Does your style work equally well with everyone, or would it be more efficient for you to use different styles when managing different personality types?

Businesses run most efficiently:

- with round pegs in round holes.

- when managers know who is round and who is square, and manage them in round and square ways; and

- by ensuring that systems mean that round and square individuals are used to complement each other and not to cause conflicts.

This can best be achieved by using some basic psychometric tests to assess personality types and preferred team roles.

One-off projects or special circumstances

These are situations that produce strains that weak management or financial controls are unable to deal with. They are, therefore, not usually the fundamental causes of failure as much as the straws that break the camel's back. Typical examples are:

- a premises move

- a big acquisition

- committing a business to a big production contract

- changing an accounting or computer system

- developing and launching a new product.

KEY POINTS

Overall, the causes of business failure are, in the main, all management issues. To avoid failure you need to:

- monitor what is happening inside and outside the business and ensure the business is managed accordingly;

- take the risks needed to ensure continued growth and returns; and

- manage your business's exposure to those risks.

HOW SERIOUS ARE YOUR PROBLEMS?

To assess how serious your problems are and whether you can save your business, complete the following checklist. Tick each strength (or its opposite weakness) that applies to your business. How balanced are your strengths/weaknesses? To what extent are the weaknesses the result of issues under your control? What overview does this give you as to how easy or difficult it is

Weaknesses	Strengths	
Management structure Weak management	Strong management	
Strategic challenges • Many causes of decline • Single plant, product, supplier or customer • Commodity product • Customers can walk away • Competitors price cutting • Industry overcapacity • Collapsing markets • Order book weak (volume and/or margin) • Weakening market position • Large capital expenditure needed • Lack of bank or shareholder support • Suppliers unco-operative • Lack of customer support	• Few causes of decline • Diversified plant, product suppliers and customers • Differentiated product • Customers locked in • Identifiable niche markets • Fragmented industry • Growing market • Strong, profitable order book • Strong market position • No major investment required • Bank and shareholder support • Co-operative suppliers • Customer support	
Financial control • Severe cash crisis • Poor financial information • Poor costing information	• Mild cash crisis • Good financial information • Good costing information	
Operational control • High fixed costs • Long-term loss contracts • Fundamental-quality problems • Old or obsolete plant and equipment	• Low fixed costs • Profitable contracts • Good-quality products • Current adequate production facilities	
One-off projects A large project being undertaken (move, acquisition or product development)	No large distraction from core business	

likely to be to turn your business around? What does this exercise suggest you are going to need to focus on to achieve this?

Remember, it is possible to try to heal the sick; it is not possible to raise the dead. If there is no reasonable prospect of saving your business, you need to consider commencing insolvency proceedings now to protect your own position (see Chapter 11).

PART 2

STABILISE YOUR FINANCES

When sales are down and costs are up, you would expect that people would concentrate on what they do actually control – cutting the costs. But that seems to fly against the entrepreneurial British business spirit.

Sir John Harvey-Jones

5

Understanding your Immediate Financial Position

WHAT YOU NEED TO KNOW

Before embarking on a turnaround, it is vital to investigate your current financial position. You need to consider the following questions:

- *How did I get here?* What has the recent trading performance been like and what are the trends?

- *Where am I now?* Are you insolvent or not? What cash do you require in the short term? To what degree can you rely on the bank?

- *Where am I going?* What are the longer-term cash, profit and loss, balance sheet and security forecasts?

If you are in a cash crisis, you have to focus on the second point before addressing the past or future so as to ensure your immediate or short-term survival.

Understanding your past financial performance is covered in Chapter 7. Short-term forecasts (which you need to prepare to obtain the proper advice on continuing to trade and to assess the immediate cash requirements and the likelihood of bank support) can be rolled forward later for use in longer-term planning.

All the workings and examples in this chapter assume you are a *director* of:

- a *limited liability company* incorporated in England and Wales

- with a number of *employees*

- that is *registered for VAT* and

- has an *overdraft* for which *the bank has taken security* by way of a valid standard UK bank debenture covering any debt due (an 'all-monies charge').

The key questions in a cash crisis are as follows:

1. *Is the company insolvent?* If it is, whilst you do not necessarily have to cease trading, there are potential implications and risks of personal liability for the directors (and shadow directors) that can arise out of your legal duties and on which you need to obtain advice (see Chapter 11).

2. *Does the company have sufficient cash for the immediate/ foreseeable future?* If not, you have just answered question 1.

3. *Will the bank* (assuming the company has bank borrowings, e.g. an overdraft) *continue to support you?* This may well determine the answer to question 2.

INSOLVENCY

In principle, insolvency simply means the company is unable to pay its debts as they fall due. Where a winding-up is sought on these grounds, the Insolvency Act 1986 sets out four tests, failure of any of which is taken to prove insolvency:

1. Failure to deal with a statutory demand.

2. Failure to pay a judgement debt.

3. The court is satisfied the company is failing to pay its debts where due ('the cashflow test').

4. The court is satisfied the company's liabilities (including contingent and prospective ones) are greater than its assets ('the balance sheet test').

Therefore both the short-term cashflow forecast and the revised balance sheet used to check the security position (covered in this chapter) are the tools you need to check the last two tests.

Insolvency matters because, if the company fails, a liquidator can potentially (see Chapter 11) act to set aside some transactions made when the company was insolvent and hold you personally liable for the company's losses. Additionally, your responsibility for the insolvency will be taken into account when considering company director disqualification proceedings (see Chapter 11). If you are not trading through a company but are acting as a sole trader, however, you have unlimited liability for all your own debts (business and personal). If you are trading in a partnership, all the partners are liable together and individually for the partnership's business liabilities ('jointly and severally'). The moral is, when in doubt, if you are concerned about solvency, you should seek professional advice.

Example
Companies D and E's balance sheets with assets stated at book value are set out below:

	Company D (£000)	**Company E** (£000)
Property	500	500
Debtors	100	100
Stock	50	50
Cash	0	0
Trade creditors	(850)	(350)
Net assets	(200)	300

No overdraft facilities have been negotiated.

Company D is clearly insolvent on a balance sheet test in that its liabilities exceed its assets. Worse still, in winding up a company, the 'going concern' basis of accounting no longer applies. This means that:

- Assets will be restated at realisable values (i.e. what they can realistically be sold for) rather than at their normal book values. Where property has been being carried in the books at its cost 25 years ago, this can be good news. More often, however, it means bad news in respect of debts, stock and work in progress, which have to be written down as what will actually be recovered.

- Liabilities must include contingent liabilities (e.g. redundancy payments to employees) that will fall due for payment ('crystallise') on failure of the company and are therefore generally higher than shown in the books.

When it comes to preparing an insolvency statement of affairs, Company D may therefore find its position is worse than it looks here on book values.

If all Company E's trade creditors are now due for payment it is insolvent on a cashflow basis as it does not have the cash to hand with which to pay these debts. Whilst it has surplus assets, its cash is largely tied up in property – an illiquid asset.

CASHFLOW FORECASTING

To assess whether you have sufficient cash for the immediate and/or foreseeable future, you need a cashflow forecast. At this stage you usually need to concentrate on the short term and prepare a forecast on a weekly basis for the next 13 weeks but, in extreme cases, you may need to prepare one on a daily basis, covering only the next few weeks.

The cashflow forecast is a vital document for the following reasons:

- It actively manages the cash to ensure survival (see Chapter 6).

- It will help you to obtain proper advice as to whether to continue to trade or not (and so protect your personal position).

- It will help in obtaining and maintaining bank support.

Cashflow forecasting is essentially straightforward as you are dealing with real cash movements into and out of the company, not abstract 'accounting' transactions, such as accruals, prepayments or depreciation.

For a weekly forecast, all you are looking to calculate are:

- the cash you are going to get *in* that week

- less the cash you are going to pay *out* that week

- to give a *net* movement ('flow') of cash into or out of your company.

Adding the net inflow (or deducting the net outflow) of cash to the balance held at the start of the week gives the balance at the end of the week, as shown below:

	Period 1	**Period 2**
	(£000)	(£000)
Cash in	100	100
Less cash out	(50)	(125)
Net cash in(out)flow	50	(25)
Balance brought forward	25	75
Balance carried forward	75	50

An example of a cashflow forecast for Company F is shown in Figure 10. This type of forecast can be set up on a spreadsheet or filled out manually, and the headings shown should be sufficient to cover the main receipts and payments of most companies.

The secret to cashflow forecasting is to keep it simple and to work methodically and logically down the page through all the cash coming in and going out of the business. For example, your *cash received* will come from the following sources:

- *Existing debtors*, who pay during the period. Look down your list of debtors, decide who is likely to pay in which week and fill in the boxes.

	Week 1 Actual	Week 2 Actual	Week 3 Actual	Week 4	Week 5	Week 6	Week 7	Week 8	Week 9	Week 10	Week 11	Week 12	Week 13	Total
Sales														
Branch 1	10,346	9,521	10,167	10,000	10,000	10,000	10,000	10,000	10,000	10,000	10,000	10,000	10,000	130,034
Branch 2	4,572	5,386	5,297	5,000	5,000	5,000	7,500	7,500	7,500	7,500	7,500	7,500	7,500	82,755
Net sales	14,918	14,907	15,464	15,000	15,000	15,000	17,500	17,500	17,500	17,500	17,500	17,500	17,500	212,789
VAT	2,611	2,609	2,706	2,625	2,625	2,625	3,063	3,063	3,063	3,063	3,063	3,063	3,063	37,238
Gross sales	17,529	17,516	18,170	17,625	17,625	17,625	20,563	20,563	20,563	20,563	20,563	20,563	20,563	250,027
Cash inflows														
Existing debtors	8,126	7,543	198	1,010										16,877
New cash sales actual	6,813	7,334	7,390											21,537
New cash sales forecast				7,050	7,050	7,050	8,225	8,225	8,225	8,225	8,225	8,225	8,225	78,725
New credit sales actual		1,026	9,386											10,412
New credit sales forecast				10,485	10,781	10,575	10,575	10,575	12,338	12,338	12,338	12,338	12,338	114,679
Any other receipts						5,200								5,200
Total inflows	14,939	15,903	16,974	18,545	17,831	22,825	18,800	18,800	20,563	20,563	20,563	20,563	20,563	247,429
Cash outflows														
Wages/salaries net				11,250				11,750					12,250	35,250
PAYE/NI – existing		4,439												4,439
PAYE/NI – new					4,500				4,650					9,150
Trade creditors – existing	10,256	9,469	10,950	11,674										42,349
New purchases					10,517	10,509	10,902	10,575	10,575	10,575	12,338	12,338	12,338	100,666
VAT – existing				15,796										15,796
VAT – new														0
Property costs (mortgage/rent/rates)				987				987				3,200	987	6,161

	1	2	3	4	5	6	7	8	9	10	11	12	13	Total
Repairs and maintenance		36		15	15	15	15	15	15	15	15	15	15	186
Utilities (heat/light/power/water)	137		369		137		369		137		369			1,518
Promotion					90							90	90	270
Telecom		436												436
Stationery	12	5	30	20	20	20	20	20	20	20	20	20	20	247
Motor vehicle running costs	156	167	170	165	165	165	165	165	165	165	200	200	200	2,388
Professional fees			3,600											3,600
Bank charges					1,200									1,200
Lease/HP/loan payments		110		110						110		200		530
Insurance	65			65				65						195
Capital expenditure						2,000								2,000
Other costs		15												15
Contingency				1,000	1,000	1,000	1,000	1,000	1,000	1,000	1,000	1,000	1,000	10,000
Total outflows	10,626	14,662	11,534	41,134	15,382	19,888	12,137	24,637	11,947	16,525	14,052	17,063	26,810	236,396
														236,396
Opening bank balance	-42,321	-38,008	-36,767	-31,327	-53,917	-51,468	-48,532	-41,869	-47,706	-39,090	-35,053	-28,542	-25,042	-42,321
Net in/(out)flows	4,313	1,241	5,440	-22,589	2,448	2,937	6,663	-5,837	8,616	4,038	6,511	3,500	-6,247	11,032
Closing bank balance	-38,008	-36,767	-31,327	-53,917	-51,468	-48,532	-41,869	-47,706	-39,090	-35,053	-28,542	-25,042	-31,289	-31,289
Bank facility available	-50,000	-50,000	-50,000	-50,000	-50,000	-50,000	-50,000	-50,000	-50,000	-50,000	-50,000	-50,000	-50,000	-50,000
Amount (over)/under facility limit	11,992	13,233	18,673	-3,917	-1,468	1,468	8,131	2,294	10,910	14,947	21,458	24,958	18,711	18,711

Fig. 10. Company F's cashflow forecast (£).

- *New sales for cash.* Prepare a simple weekly sales forecast by branch, line of business, contract, customer or whatever is most appropriate. Then calculate how much of these sales will be for cash (in Company F's case, 40%) and fill in the boxes (remembering to add VAT as your receipts will be gross).

- *New sales on credit*, where the customer pays within the forecast period. Once you have forecast sales, those that are not for cash must be made on credit. How long a credit period are you allowing your customers, and how long are they really taking to pay? For Company F it is broadly two weeks. Use this as a guide to plotting the likely weekly receipts from these new sales (again gross of VAT).

- *Any other sources.* Will you be selling any assets, injecting any new funds, receiving any insurance payouts, like Company F, or generating any other cash from anywhere at all? If so, estimate how much and in which week (don't forget VAT where it applies), and enter the figures.

You can now total all these to obtain your estimated total weekly inflows. Outflows are calculated on exactly the same principles. Do you pay the wages weekly or monthly? Write in the net amounts when they will go out. PAYE is due once a month, VAT at the end of the month following the end of the quarter, so predicting the dates of these payments should be straightforward.

Your purchase ledger/trade creditor list also tells you whom you owe money to for purchases. So in the same way you forecast receipts from debtors, go down the list and plan when you are going to pay what to whom. Bear in mind you will also need to continue to make purchases as you trade, so forecast these in the same way as you forecast sales and plan in the payments (gross of VAT) for when you are going to make them.

You will need to plan payments for rent, heating, lighting, power, telephone and your other commitments in the same way, as well as remembering to estimate how much VAT will need to be paid, and when.

The keys to successful cashflow forecasting are:

Know where you are starting from

As you stand today you have a balance at the bank; you are owed money by your debtors you are expecting to receive; and you will owe money to trade creditors, the Inland Revenue, HM Customs & Excise and so on. Use these figures as your opening balances. If you do not have exact figures (why not?) use your best estimates.

Make sure you are consistent

Try to forecast the balance that will be shown on your bank statement rather than that which will show in your cashbook, as this will give you the most useful information. Enter the current balance from your bank statement as your starting bank balance and add back all those cheques sitting in the drawer or unpresented to your opening creditor figure so as to show how much you really owe.

Be realistic in your estimates of timings and amounts

Your forecast needs to take into account the following:

• What level are sales/purchases running at now?

• What changes are really likely to happen over the period?

• What have you experienced in prior periods? (How quickly do your customers actually pay?)

• What are your terms of trade? (What length of credit do you allow customers/are you allowed by suppliers?)

• What are your due dates for statutory payments? (For example, the 19th of the month for PAYE.)

• What are your periodic payments? (For example, quarterly bills for utilities and rent.)

• What capital expenditure are you planning?

When in doubt be prudent

Be pessimistic about when and how much people are going to
pay you, and about when you are going to have to pay others.

Make your assumptions explicit

If you tell your bank manager sales are going to increase by
20% the week after next, you can then also tell him or her this is
because your contract with XYZ plc comes on stream.
Otherwise the manager may just think you are relying on the
'new sales fairy' to wave a wand and make this happen.

Check that you are showing all aspects of any transaction

Company F has taken on a new sales representative for branch 2
(wages and PAYE go up). It is buying a new van for this
representative (a deposit is shown as capital expenditure and a
new monthly HP charge), which will require fuel (motor vehicle
expenses). Of course the reason for doing so is to increase sales
and hence debtor receipts, but these will also be reflected in
increased purchases and, hence, payments for goods sold.

Experiment with sensitivities

Flex some of your key assumptions (what if sales go up by 5%
instead of 10%; what if customers take 60 days to pay instead of
45?) to see how sensitive the forecast is to these fluctuations.
Make sure you reflect fully all aspects of any change, however.
But remember the above point: if sales go down, purchases
should fall as well.

Think widely

Check you have allowed for all possible payments that may
need to be made by comparing the type of items with last year's
detailed profit and loss account. Have you allowed for
corporation tax, redundancy payments, pension top-ups or

repairs if any of these are likely to fall due in the period? Turnarounds tend to require professional assistance. Have you allowed sufficient to cover the accountants, lawyers and bankers' fees? Go through some old bank statements and cheque-book stubs. Have you allowed for all types of payment you find?

Check carefully to make sure it all adds up

Company F's cashflow forecast has 'check totals' built in at the end. These are simply sums that add up the elements of the forecast in different ways to ensure nothing has been left out. An example of the principle is illustrated in Figure 11, where the first 9 is calculated by adding together the values of all the column totals. The second 9 is calculated by adding all the row totals. If the two check sum totals match, you can be confident there are unlikely to be any basic arithmetic errors in the forecast.

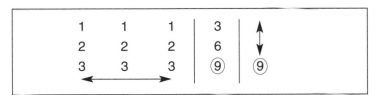

Fig. 11. Checking the arithmetic in the cashflow forecast.

Build in margins for errors

Build in a margin as a round sum contingency to allow for the things that will inevitably come crawling out of the woodwork. The more uncertain your starting point, the larger this needs to be, up to, say, 10% or 20% of payments in some cases.

Part of the reason for cashflow forecasting is to build the bank's confidence you are in control of your finances. Having a contingency in place is not only prudent, but if it helps ensure you beat your forecast cash performance, it will also help to ensure the bank's confidence in your management skills will increase.

Example

The technique can also be used to review any large contract or project a company is planning to undertake. Company G is a roofing business at the limits of its overdraft and it receives news it has won a large contract, the details of which are as follows:

Contract value	£620K
Subcontracted labour	£300K at £50K per month over six months
Materials	£200K, of which £100K is required in the first month, followed by £20K per month for five months
Giving a profit of	£120K

Whilst the company has one month's credit from its suppliers for materials, it has to pay labour monthly (but labour is paid gross with no PAYE deductions). There is no retention on the contract and the company is to bill at the end of each month for the materials delivered, labour and one sixth of the profit, and the client will pay at the end of 30 days. The directors are jubilant and are convinced this is going to save the company. Undoubtedly, it is a profitable contract. But should the company take it? The answer lies in looking at the cashflow (to simplify matters, VAT has been omitted):

Projected project cashflow (£000) per month

	1	2	3	4	5	6	7	8
Receipts	—	—	170	90	90	90	90	90
Payments								
Labour	50	50	50	50	50	50	—	—
Materials	—	100	20	20	20	20	20	—
Total payments	50	150	70	70	70	70	20	
Net movement (out)/inflow	(50)	(150)	100	20	20	20	70	90
Cumulative	(50)	(200)	(100)	(80)	(60)	(40)	30	120

The answer, then, is clearly no – not as it stands. The project's early cash outflows mean the company, which is at the edge of its facility, will immediately run out of cash if it accepts the contract and starts work.

Instead, Company G must explore whether the proposed payment terms can be changed to speed up receipt of cash (e.g. an upfront payment), whether greater credit can be obtained from the labour and material suppliers and/or whether it can negotiate increased facilities with the bank to enable the project to be undertaken.

Once you have prepared your forecast, use what you have produced.

Review it critically

Having prepared your forecast on a prudent basis, now see what scope there is for moving payments or for bringing forward receipts. Compare the balance at the end of each week with the facility you have with the bank. Do you have 'headroom' or are you going to be in 'excess'?

Use your forecast to plan

If you are going to be in excess, plan what you are going to do about it (see Chapter 6). Look at what payments or receipts you can change and/or speak to the bank in advance about the excess to agree a temporary extra facility. Use the cashflow forecast to explain why the excess will occur, how much it will be, how long it will be for and for explaining how you are going to reduce your borrowing to return to your normal facility.

As a word of caution, however, don't run to the bank with your first draft cashflow forecast as this is likely to show a dreadful cash position (you have been pessimistic after all). Only discuss your forecast with your bank once you have had a chance to review it thoroughly to amend and adjust it for the things you are realistically going to be able to manage to improve the position. You need to discuss a final working forecast that is challenging but realistic and prudent, not ultra-pessimistic.

Use your forecast to monitor

Roll the forecast forwards, week after week, comparing what
actually happens to your forecast. Ask yourself where they
differed and why. Then ask what that tells you about your
estimates going forward and where you can/should amend
your forecast to improve your estimates. From Company F's
actual results in weeks 1–3, it seems the contingency built in is
too high as the only sundry expense has been the milkman at
£15!

SUPPORT FROM THE BANK

Banks tend to support customers in difficulties when the
following conditions are met:

- The bank trusts your integrity.

- You talk to the bank in time (and seem likely to continue to
  talk to them).

- You seem to be in control of your business (and its numbers).

- You have a plan.

- The plan sets out clearly what support you need (how much,
  how long, how it is to be paid back).

- You are prepared to get in help where you need it.

- The bank is confident your plan can work.

- The bank is confident you can make it happen.

- Your plan does not materially increase the bank's risk.

However, you need to understand the bank's perspective. If you
were a banker, whom would you be prepared to lend money to?
Essentially the answer is: someone you were confident was
likely to repay you. After all, it takes a great deal of interest
income from loans at 2% over the cost to the bank of borrowing
the money to claw back a lost loan. But what makes a bank
confident that its loans to a company are going to be repaid?
   The bank has to judge its confidence in your ability to use

that money sensibly and to control your business. If your business needs a turnaround, particularly when it has reached a crisis, the bank's confidence in you is likely to be significantly reduced. You will have to take action to demonstrate you know and are in control of what is happening in your business (e.g. robust cashflow forecasting) and that you can take tough decisions (e.g. on cutting costs or staff) to restore the bank's confidence.

But even if the bank has confidence in your integrity and abilities, if you are needing to turnaround your business, by definition, it is in some kind of trading difficulty. So, how keen would you be to lend your money to a business in difficulty? What questions would you ask? The principles involved when your company borrows money from a bank are exactly the same as when you, as an individual, borrow money to buy a house. When you apply for a mortgage, the lender wants to know two things before they grant a mortgage:

1. *What you earn* so they can see that your stream of income (*your cashflow*) is enough to allow you to make the payments. For a company, your cashflow and profit and loss forecasts are estimates of future earnings on which the bank will need to judge whether sufficient money is going to be made to repay the loan. In the case of a company in difficulty, the projections are going to come under sceptical scrutiny and therefore need to be well thought through, robust and realistic.

2. *What is the value of the property compared to the loan* so that if you cannot pay they will be able to take possession of the house (*their security*) and sell it for enough to recover their loan.

Example
Mr H buys a house for £100K. His bank is happy to lend him 80% of the value on a mortgage (£80K). Three years later, Mr H has paid off £5K in capital and the house has risen in value by 50%. The bank's security position has improved by £55K:

	Initial (£000)	Current (£000)
Property at current realisable value	100	150
Outstanding loan	(80)	(75)
Surplus security	20	75
Loan to value ratio	80%	50%

In the housing market, this surplus is usually referred to as 'equity'.

The statement in the example ignores any costs of realisation (e.g. estate agent fees). Whilst these costs can be significant (particularly in the case of a company), for the purposes of estimating security on an ongoing basis, banks usually ignore these costs to keep the tracking and calculation of security cover simple. In a crisis however, costs start to be considered in more detail and can affect the bank's view of the value of its security.

For a company that has a variety of assets and liabilities, the position is more complex than that of an individual taking out a mortgage to buy a single asset, but the principles are the same. For our purposes, the steps required to calculate a basic security statement so as to understand the bank's exposure are as follows:

1. Obtain an up-to-date balance sheet (a statement of assets and liabilities).

2 Reorder the assets and liabilities according to their relative priorities.

3. Restate the assets at realisable values.

4. Identify and net off certain specific liabilities.

5. Apply debenture values.

The easiest way to demonstrate these steps is by the use of a worked example

Obtaining an up-to-date balance sheet – example

The following is an extract from Company H's balance sheet where the bank has a standard UK bank charge ('debenture'):

Company H's balance sheet		£000	£000
Fixed assets			
Land and buildings		20	
Plant and machinery		100	120
Current assets			
Debtors		200	
Stock	Finished goods	50	
	Work in progress	50	
	Raw materials	50	350
Current liabilities			
Trade creditors		(100)	
HP		(10)	
PAYE		(20)	
VAT		(10)	
Overdraft		(200)	(340)
Net assets			130

The company has net assets, so you might think the bank would feel secure. However, to check this we need to produce an estimated security position statement by applying the steps set out above.

Reordering assets and liabilities

A normal UK bank debenture will give the bank 'fixed' and 'floating' charges. Assets must therefore be divided into those subject to the bank's fixed charge (generally land and buildings and debtors) and all the other assets, which will be covered by a floating charge. If it has to call on its security, the bank will be paid out first from the net proceeds of sale of the *fixed charge assets*.

The debenture will probably state that plant and machinery are covered by a fixed charge but, in general, this will not be effective and therefore plant and machinery come under the floating charge. If, however, the bank has taken a chattel mortgage over specific listed items of plant and machinery, these items should be included under the fixed charge.

The proceeds of sale of the *floating charge assets* are used, first, to settle certain creditors (known as the preferential creditors), which are, broadly the following:

* *PAYE/NI* due in respect of the last *twelve months*.

* *VAT* in respect of the last *six* months.

* *Employees' wages* of up to £800 per month for the last *four* months (but not redundancy).

Only when the preferential creditors have been paid is any surplus cash paid to the bank. And only when the bank's lending has been settled are any funds available for all the other creditors ('unsecured creditors').

Restating assets at realisable values

Realistically, and for the purposes of most discussions with banks, this need only be done for land and buildings where book values are based on original costs and these figures may be wildly different from actual current value. In Company H's case the property is recorded in the books at its cost of many years ago of £20K (book value). However, as the property is currently worth £80K, this is the value that will need to be shown in the security statement.

If your bank becomes sufficiently concerned to send in investigating accountants, part of their report to the bank will be a detailed security position statement. They will most probably look closely at likely realisable values (e.g. have property and plant and machinery professionally valued on the relevant 'forced sale' basis).

Identifying and netting off certain specific liabilities

Creditors fall into one of three general categories for the purposes of deciding where they rank in order of priority to be paid: secured creditors with fixed or floating charges, preferential creditors and unsecured creditors. There are, however, some specific items to be wary of.

Where plant and machinery is held under HP or a lease, it is not actually the company's property. Nevertheless, if the value of the plant exceeds the HP or lease liability, this surplus value ('equity') will be available to the bank as you can pay off the HP, sell the assets and realise the difference in cash. So for Company H, the £10K HP liability will need to be deducted from the value of the assets to achieve a net amount of assets available for the bank.

If the outstanding HP is greater than the value of the assets, the net value of the plant and machinery available to the bank should be shown as nil. Any apparent deficit suffered by the HP company would be added to unsecured creditors.

Similarly, if you factor or invoice discount your debts, the amount due to the factors/invoice discounters must be deducted from the debtors to work out the net available to the bank as your factors/invoice discounters will have negotiated a fixed charge over debtors, giving them priority over the bank.

Applying debenture values

In the same way a bank will normally lend, say, only 80% of a property's value when giving you a mortgage, so it will only lend certain percentages against different classes of assets ('debenture values'). Some typical examples are given in Figure 12.

Asset	Debenture value	Comment
Land and buildings	75%–80%	The banks' favourite form of security.
Debtors	50%	If there are significant balances due over three months old, they may be discounted when valuing security. Debts in respect of stage payments on long-term contracts (such as in the construction industry) are treated very cautiously by banks. This is due to the potential for counter-claims by customers in the event of non-completion of work by a failed company. They may, therefore, have a much lower debenture value.

Asset	Debenture value	Comment
Plant and machinery	20%	But may vary significantly depending on the nature of the plant, the ease with which it can be recovered/sold and how active a second-hand market there is. Given its rapid obsolescence, computer equipment, for example, has a low debenture value.
Finished goods stock	Up to 50%	Depends on the nature of the stock. Pencils would be easily realisable at near normal price. Complex specialist equipment, however, might be difficult to sell without a meaningful warranty to support it.
Work in progress	Usually nil	Unless it can be sold to someone who can finish it off. In construction, the key will be: can the contracts be transferred to another company to complete?
Raw materials	Possibly 20–40%	Depends on the nature of the stock. However, suppliers will often have reservation of title claims over unprocessed supplies which will need to be resolved to obtain a complete picture.

Fig. 12. Debenture values.

Example
The result of applying these rules to Company H's balance sheet is a security position statement that shows the following:

	Value	Debenture percentage (£000)	Security value (£000)
Assets subject to a fixed charge			
Land and buildings	80	75%	60
Debtors	200	50%	100
			160
Less due to bank			(200)
Surplus/(deficit)			(40)

Assets subject to a floating charge

Plant and machinery		100	20%	20
Less HP		—		(10)
Stock	Finished goods	50	40%	20
	Work in progress	50	—	—
	Raw materials	50	20%	10
				40

Less preferential creditors

PAYE/NI	(20)		
VAT	(10)		(30)

Available for the bank	10
Bank deficit from above	(40)
Bank surplus/(deficit)	(30)
Available for all other creditors	0

As things stand, therefore, the bank is facing a deficit on its security in the event of a liquidation or receivership, before allowing for the costs of realisation. If as a director of Company H you have personally guaranteed the borrowings, you should also be concerned as, in the event of a shortfall, the bank can call on you to make good their loss. There is also clearly nothing in the pot for the £100K of unsecured trade creditors, or for any employee redundancy claims or other contingent liabilities (e.g. future warranty claims).

Whilst a full estimate of a bank's security position is a complex matter, requiring specialist assistance in the valuation of assets and in assessing reservation of title clauses, this approach should provide you with a sufficient basis to understand and to discuss with your bank how confident or exposed they feel about your business.

Unfortunately at the time of writing the situation has become confused as the result of the decision in a case called Brumark which suggests that some bank fixed charges over book debts may be ineffective and will only operate as floating charges. If upheld this will significantly affect this type of security calculation so you should check the current position with a professional advisor.

By rolling forward your balance sheet for the forecast period, you can also see how the bank's security position is likely to be affected by further trading. Also, by establishing whether you are asking your bank to become more exposed or whether your action will help your bank to improve its position, you will be putting yourself in a situation where you can ask for your bank's support.

KEY POINTS

- Can you pay your debts as they fall due? If not, you are insolvent. Don't panic, but do get professional advice.

- Work out how much cash you are going to need in the short term. This is the first step towards making sure you have it.

- Work out how comfortable/exposed the bank is, and will become, before you sit down to talk to them about how much cash you need.

- Use the tools discussed in this chapter to help you keep track as you progress.

6

Managing a Real Cash Crisis

WEALTH WARNING

You must not simply use the techniques outlined in this chapter
to obtain more cash, particularly by increasing your borrowings
or by taking further credit to stave off an inevitable collapse. If
you do, as a director you will be running risks of personal
liability for wrongful or even, possibly, fraudulent trading (see
Chapter 11).

The purpose of this chapter is to help you to weather a cash
crisis in order to put a turnaround plan into place, with some
reasonable chance of success. If you are in a cash crisis and you
have (or it would be reasonable to have) any concerns about
whether there is any prospect of the business surviving, you
must take professional advice to protect your personal position.

ACHIEVING BALANCE

In a cash crisis, your business's short-term survival depends on
you taking emergency measures to conserve and generate cash
to buy time for longer-term issues to be addressed. Unfortunately, you may need to take action before making a full
assessment of your business's problems or before deciding on
your recovery strategy. There is, therefore, always a risk that the
short-term actions you take will be detrimental to your
business's long-term interests.

While surviving the short term must take priority at this stage
in order to have a long term future to worry about, where
possible you should try to consider the long-term consequences
and should adopt an approach that balances short-term survival
with long-term regeneration.

Unnecessarily closing the factory you will need for your long-
term recovery as part of your short-term cost-cutting plan tends
to look not too clever in hindsight. But if it is a case of close the

factory or go out of business, don't hesitate – close the factory! Remember, you will not be around to worry about implementing your turnaround plan unless you have enough cash to pay the wages and suppliers this week and the next.

THE KEY STEPS TO SURVIVAL

A cash crisis can arise for a number of reasons, ranging from operating losses or the servicing of excessive debts draining the cash away to excessive capital expenditure or inefficient trading operations absorbing too much cash into illiquid assets, through to too high a rate of growth where the supply of cash is too slow.

To survive a cash crisis you must focus on some or all of the following key areas, although the steps you need to take will be determined by the underlying cause of the cash shortage:

1. Control the cash you have.

2. Get in more cash from normal trading.

3. Get in more cash or credit from elsewhere.

4. Reduce and/or control the cash going out.

5. Reduce the amount of cash you need to trade.

6. Improve profits.

7. Improve management.

Generally, the first five areas have quicker effects than the last two, and your cashflow forecast will show how pressing the crisis is.

One way to prioritise actions is to use a matrix such as the one shown in Figure 13 to plot your estimates of which actions will have the largest/fastest relative effects so you can focus on the ones that will make a real difference.

If you can demonstrate you can identify, face up to and deal with a severe cash crisis by taking the actions necessary to survive, you will increase your credibility with stakeholders (particularly your bank).

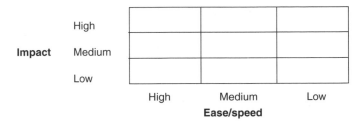

	High			
Impact	Medium			
	Low			
		High	Medium	Low

Ease/speed

Fig. 13. Prioritising actions.

CONTROLLING THE CASH YOU HAVE

It is surprising how many businesses that are in a cash crisis fail
to take the basic steps to control this scarcest of resources and to
ensure it is used as efficiently as possible. First, prepare a
cashflow forecast. From this exercise it will follow logically
that, to manage the business's cash efficiently, you should take
the following steps:

* *Centralise the control of cash receipts, payments and
  forecasting* (and forecast daily on a cleared funds at bank
  basis). You can then prioritise and schedule payments so the
  available cash is best used for the benefit of the whole
  business rather than being used, say, by individual managers,
  sites or branches as they see fit.

* *Roll forward the cashflow forecast on a regular basis,*
  reviewing performance against forecast each time you do so
  to pick up any variances that need to be investigated or that
  can be used to improve the next forecast's accuracy.

* *Increase the level of authority required for purchasing or
  payments.* Credit/charge cards should usually be cancelled or
  restricted so that cash is not wasted or committed outside the
  central forecasting regime.

* By preparing a cashflow forecast you may be able to *identify
  where the cash is leaking out.* Is it particular branches, sites
  or parts of the business? If so, target these areas for specific
  reviews and remedial action.

OBTAINING MORE CASH FROM NORMAL TRADING

You are likely to have a great deal of money tied up in debtors. As trading and sales become more difficult, many businesses feel less confident in demanding payment from customers for fear of losing future business, or are distracted from the day-to-day necessity of chasing in debts and, by default, they allow debtors to enjoy longer or more extensive credit terms than normal. This ties up vital working capital and is often the first place to look for funds.

Review the debtors ledger and take action to reduce credit terms to customers and to target and get in overdue debts. If as a result you find that credit control procedures or practices are poor, mark this as an area for specific action as part of your turnaround plan. In the mean time, introduce tougher credit terms for customers.

OBTAINING MORE CASH OR CREDIT FROM ELSEWHERE

Other than trading, possible sources of cash include selling assets, raising new borrowings or obtaining investment. Review the assets on your balance sheet to identify the following:

- Surplus fixed assets (land and buildings, plant and machinery, motor vehicles) that can be sold.

- Assets that could, potentially, be made surplus (and then sold) e.g. by subcontracting out your manufacturing processes.

- Essential fixed assets that can be sold and leased back to provide cash while still being used.

- Underutilised plant and machinery capacity that can be hired out, or spare factory or office space that could be sublet.

- Separable and saleable investments, subsidiaries or any parts of your business (e.g. a specific branch).

Is there any equipment lying around (that might not even be on the balance sheet) that can be sold? Can you use asset-based financing (including factoring or discounting your debts) to obtain more borrowings against your assets than are available from your bank under its debenture values? (See the discussion of security in Chapter 5 or try www.creativefinance.co.uk). Do you have any unpledged assets that can provide security for new loans, such as brands, trademarks and other intellectual property rights?

Using your cashflow forecast, seek to negotiate an extension of your existing bank facilities or other borrowings to cover the forecast requirement. If appropriate, seek to agree deferment of loan repayments or to roll up interest for later payment. If seeking to borrow further funds, always consider carefully your business's ability to meet the payments in both the short and long term before taking further money. You do not want to dig yourself deeper into debt you cannot afford to service.

Agree new stocking arrangements with supportive creditors (such as sale or return or pay when paid) or agree longer payment terms. Ask customers to supply free issue stock for you to work on so you do not have to buy in materials. Seek injections of capital from shareholders or directors (the bank may well put pressure on you for this to happen in any event as a sign of your commitment to the turnaround, as well as to reduce its exposure).

If you are asked to make a further investment in a business in difficulty or to guarantee personally further borrowings for a company, it goes without saying that you must look very carefully at the commitment you are making, the likelihood of recovery and the impact it will have on you should the business fail. You should always consider getting professional advice in these circumstances.

REDUCING AND/OR CONTROLLING OUTGOING CASH

As with all things in life, what we don't spend, we keep. Cancel discretionary expenditure, such as the payments of dividends. Cut back or cancel the following:

- *Advertising/marketing*, but assess how immediate the link is between this and sales and do not cut advertising that is vital for short-term turnover.

- *Training*, but retain any training necessary to meet statutory requirements.

- *Research and development*, but assess the risk you may run of losing any key projects or staff that are vital to the long-term recovery plan.

- *Capital expenditure*, but assess how vital any such planned expenditure is to improving profitability in the short term or to the long-term turnaround plan.

Increase creditor payment periods through agreement with suppliers. Negotiate scheduled payments with your key creditors, the Inland Revenue and HM Customs & Excise (an 'informal arrangement'). If agreeing scheduled payments with suppliers, be clear as to what proportion of the payments made is going to be used by the supplier to reduce the total amount you owe and what proportion will be used to allow further supplies on credit.

Consider using an Insolvency Act procedure (see Chapter 2) to obtain protection or agree a formal binding deal with creditors. (Try www.turnaroundhelp.co.uk for a local advisor). Consider whether any key creditors might be willing to convert their debt to shares in the business ('debt for equity swap'), if this is acceptable to the existing shareholders. In the right circumstances, some banks will consider such steps. Others will not.

Pensions

In the aftermath of the Maxwell affair, the regulations to protect employees' pensions have become more stringent, with strict duties and timescales imposed on companies to pay employer and employee pension contributions to the relevant pension schemes.

The different types of pension schemes in operation today make this a complex area, but the following general rules must be applied: always pay over employee contributions deducted from salaries and always obtain professional advice on any proposal to reduce employer contributions *before* making any change.

REDUCING THE AMOUNT OF CASH NEEDED TO TRADE

Your 'working capital cycle' should be a virtuous circle (see Figure 14). Whether your working capital cycle requires funding is determined by your actual terms of trade with suppliers and customers. Reducing the cash tied up in the cycle means that what cash you do have can fund more trading.

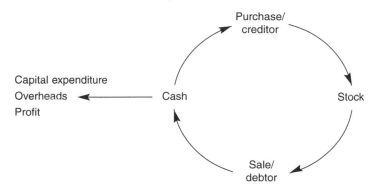

Fig. 14. The working capital cycle.

Example
Company J deals with only one item at a time, and its current transactions are summarised below:

01/01	Purchases a widget for £100 on one month's credit
31/01	Pays supplier for widget
28/02	Sells widget at 200% mark-up on one month's credit after normal two months in stock
31/03	Customer pays £300

Plotting these transactions over time we can show how the borrowing requirement to fund this working capital cycle is £100 over two months (Figure 15). A bank will see this as an appropriate use of an overdraft facility, which will swing back into credit as the transaction unwinds into realised profit and cash. However, in practice, Company J will need to agree the facility in advance with the bank and it will need to offer some other security (such as personal guarantees) as the bank will be unlikely to lend against 100% of stock value without this.

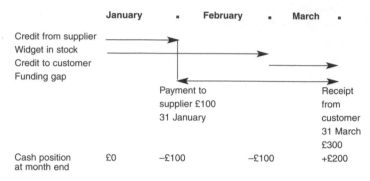

Fig. 15. Company J: borrowing requirement.

You can also see that Company J could reduce its borrowing requirements to nil by changing its trading arrangements. For example, it could reduce its investment in stock and debtors:

- If it bought in the widget only when it had a firm order and could ship it straight out (a 'back to back' deal), the debtor would pay at exactly the same time as the creditor was due.

- If it stocked only what it could sell in a month for cash.

It might also replace bank lending with supplier credit by taking three months' credit that would match the date of receipt and payment. It could also adapt a mixture of these two approaches, e.g. take two months' credit from suppliers and stock only items that sell in a month.

Even if it implemented any of these, Company J should still negotiate a bank facility as insurance against any unforeseen cashflow problems.

You should look at all aspects of your working capital to see where there is scope for a reduction:

- *Reduce finished goods stock* (e.g. by a sale of slow-moving or old items), but be careful with such strategies and consider the risks and consequences (e.g. is dumping stock in your normal markets going to spoil your efforts to increase normal sales?).

- *Complete work in progress* and turn it into sellable, finished goods as soon as possible.

- *Review your production management,* particularly if you are building, say, batches of subassemblies. Does this mean you are deliberately tying up cash in parts that will not become finished goods for a long time? Can you move to just-in-time production?

- *Cancel or reduce any outstanding raw material orders,* as long as this does not give you a contractual problem or unacceptable risks of stock-outs.

- *Return any unnecessary stockholdings to suppliers,* either by agreement or by stepping up your quality control standards and checks.

IMPROVING PROFITS

To improve profits fundamentally requires achieving some combination of the following, depending on which area is most responsible for the problem:

- *Increasing turnover* by increasing some or all of customer numbers, value of spend per customer or frequency of spend.

- *Increasing margins* by reducing costs of sales.

- And/or *reducing overheads,* including dealing with any non-performing parts of the business that are dragging the rest of the business down.

In a cash crisis, the short-term practical steps tend to focus on cost reduction.

Increasing turnover

Can you raise prices? However, first check how sensitive your sales volume will be to price. If you produce a 'commodity' (e.g. pencils), customers will tend to buy largely on price. As they can obtain exactly the same thing from Joe down the road if he is cheaper, raising prices above market rates will lead to a major loss of sales. If your product or service is 'differentiated' (where customers cannot buy exactly the same thing from Joe), the position is a more complex question of perceived value, and you must judge how much you can increase your price before customers decide that Joe's cheaper product will do well enough for their needs.

What opportunities can you identify to increase volumes quickly, cost effectively and relatively certainly by attracting more customers, getting them to come back more often or to spend more while they are buying from you (e.g. do your staff ask whether customers want a new oil filter when they come in to buy oil)?

Increasing margins

Identify the key constraints on your business (e.g. we only have one XYZ machine, which is a production bottleneck) and ensure that profit is maximised for that constraint (i.e. we should seek orders for product 1 as we make more money per hour of XYZ machine operation than we do by producing product 2).

Improve your productivity/output by looking at your processes, but solutions requiring capital expenditure (e.g. increased automation) tend to be long-term issues.

Improve your efficiency in your control of purchasing, distribution, contract control, quality assurance or waste management. Look for any opportunities to reduce the cost of goods sold (e.g. reduce raw material prices, reduce scrap, change materials, lower the labour component).

Reduce wage costs by introducing short-time working or a redundancy programme (compare your head count to competitors' or to that of two or three years ago), but be careful to ensure this is understood to be a short-term step and do not preclude the need to make further long-term changes.

Redundancies

When making redundancies you must meet current standards and legislation in respect of:

* consultation with employees
* the grounds for redundancy
* the selection of employees.

It is best, therefore, to obtain up-to-date advice from your solicitor. You will also need to fund any redundancy payments required. In some circumstances, the DTI's redundancy fund will be able to grant you a loan with which to fund the payments, and you should contact the DTI to find out what assistance is currently available.

Reducing overheads

Can you reduce manufacturing overheads? Are your selling, general and administrative expenses in line with industry standards? Can you look for savings in some of the following areas:

* *Management salaries* – should you 'share the pain'?
* *Premises costs* – can you consolidate and lease out extra space?
* *Vehicles* – can you eliminate the car fleet or have your employees bear the costs of cars?
* *Professional costs* – can you reduce the costs of accountants, lawyers, etc.?
* *Postage* – do you really need overnight couriers, etc.?
* *Telephone costs.*
* *Advertising and promotion costs* – is your advertising cost effective? Is it an investment in the future or a necessary expense for obtaining sales in the short term?
* *Selling expenses* – can you cut the size of the sales force or

the number of sales offices without significant short-term costs?

Consider closing or selling any of your business' subsidiaries or branches that have net cash outflows or that are unprofitable (but see Chapter 7). Rationalise your customers, products, prices, processes and funding.

IMPROVING MANAGEMENT

You need to look at whether you need further management expertise. Do you need a finance director to:

- Provide strong guidance in respect of your strategy?
- Provide financial advice on major decisions?
- Liaise with your bank?
- Prepare regular cashflow forecasts and budgets, including profit and loss accounts and balance sheets?
- Assist in preparation of feasibility studies on major development projects?
- Integrate accounting systems as required and install adequate internal controls?
- Plan your tax strategy to minimise tax costs?
- Oversee the company secretarial functions?

Do you need to change your management structure, incentivisation or culture (see Chapter 10)?

7

Understanding and Controlling your Financial Performance

WHAT YOU NEED TO KNOW

So far we have looked at short-term cash issues; what generates cash in the long term, however, is profit. This chapter there fore attempts to demystify the terms surrounding financial information and, in so doing, to show how you can use financial information to understand and control your business.

The two key areas you should measure and understand are profitability and financial stability. *Profitability* includes the types of costs you incur; gross profit, contribution and break-even; profit improvement; and cost drivers. *Financial stability* considers liquidity and gearing.

The keys to using financial information, therefore, are as follows. You should:

- use profit centres;
- control and analyse cost trends;
- use cost information;
- quantify management decisions;
- use management accounts;
- monitor returns; and
- monitor your working capital cycle.

Having measured your performance, it is important to realise that the absolute results for any company at any particular date tend to be less important than the use of the information to measure trends over time (e.g. growth) and to benchmark performance against others. You should also appreciate that financial figures are produced as a result of what you are doing to run the business. They are the symptoms and evidence of what is happening, not the cause of what is happening.

However, once you are measuring your financial performance you can set financial targets for your business (e.g. reducing your average debtor payment time to 45 days by the end of the first quarter) as part of your plan and can use this financial information to monitor your progress. And the actions you will have to take to make these financial results appear will be *real* actions in the *real* world, such as setting tight credit terms for your customers, issuing statements, picking up the telephone to chase in the money when it is due and putting customers on stop if they don't pay.

PROFITABILITY

Profitability means measuring whether you are making any money, finding out what you are spending money on and understanding how much business you need to have in order to make a profit.

Types of costs

To understand your profitability, you must understand your cost structure. There are various types of costs for any business (see Figure 16). Fixed costs are, of course, not fixed in the long term (you can move factory or hire and fire factory staff) and will eventually reflect levels of production and activity. A profit and loss account, however will only divide costs into two broad areas:

1. Costs of sales (CoS) which will include all variable direct costs.
2. Overheads, which will include all fixed indirect costs.

Businesses differ as to how they categorise direct fixed costs as either cost of sales or overheads. If you do not include all your direct fixed costs in calculating your cost of sales, you risk underestimating your costs when it comes to setting prices or tendering for contracts. The result of continuously selling at less than your true cost of manufacture (i.e. at a loss) is, inevitably, failure. It is generally best, therefore, to include your direct costs as fully as possible in establishing your cost of sales.

	Variable (the level of cost varies directly with the level of production)	**Fixed** (fixed costs do not vary in the short term as production fluctuates)
Direct costs: relate directly to the cost of producing goods for sale	• raw materials • piecework wages • overtime pay • factory energy costs	• normal factory wages • machinery costs and depreciation • factory rent
Indirect costs: general costs of being in business that are not directly related to particular costs of production		• auditors' fees • sales staff wages • directors' fees

Fig. 16. Types of cost.

If your production volumes swing significantly between periods, however, you will need to be careful in using cost of sales to establish a meaningful 'contribution' figure for sales, and you may find it best to treat all fixed costs as overheads for the purpose of calculating break-even levels.

Gross profit and break-even

The first important profit figures are your gross profit and gross profit percentage as these are used to calculate break-even.

Example
Company K sells each of its widgets for £150. Its cost of sales per widget are:

Raw materials (£50)
Labour and manufacturing costs (£50)

Its gross profit per widget, therefore, is £50. Based on gross profit/sales, its gross profit percentage is 33.3% or £50/£150.

Company K has overheads of £1,000 per month. As its gross profit per widget (or 'contribution' towards covering overheads) is £50 per widget, it has to sell 20 widgets a month (£1,000/£50) before the total contribution is sufficient to cover all the overheads, (or to 'break even').

Its break-even turnover is therefore £3,000 per month (£150 x 20).

This break-even has used 'accounting figures' based on costs taken from the profit and loss accounts. However it is often useful to redo this exercise to calculate a 'cash break-even' stripping out the key costs that do not represent cash (e.g. depreciation) and replacing this with the real cash item (e.g. lease payments).

Example
Company K's overheads include a £100 depreciation charge and a £50 HP interest charge per month. The HP payment per month is in fact, £250 (£50 interest and £200 'capital' payment). So Company K's overheads restated on a cash basis are as follows:

	£
Overheads	1,000
Less Depreciation	(100)
Add Capital payment	200
	1,100

As a result, its break-even turnover on a cash basis is 22 widgets or £3,300 per month.

Profit improvement

As you start to consider break-even calculations, something becomes very clear. To improve profits, you can do any or all of three things:

1. Increase turnover.
2. Increase margins (gross profit percentage).
3. Reduce overheads.

And if you can do all three, the effects multiply.

Example

Company L (10% improvements)

Turnover	£1,000	+ £100	£1,100
Gross profit (%)	50	+ 5	55
Gross profit	500		605
Overheads	(250)	-25	(225)
Profit	250		380 = 52% increase

Cost drivers

The relative level of your costs compared to your competitors' will be the result of a number of factors, the most common of which are listed below. Look at the opportunities to reduce costs in each of these areas but be alert to the common pitfalls of poorly applied cost reductions – for example, where disruptions and other problems outweigh the planned saving:

• Economies of scale (sometimes bigger is better).

• Capacity utilisation (you are paying for that plant and those people, whether they are earning for you or not).

• Learning curves (the more you do, the better at it you become).

• Location (relative local costs and transportation costs).

• Purchasing (how good at buying are you?).

• Operating efficiency.

• Investment (e.g. in automation or training).

• Waste management.

FINANCIAL STABILITY

Liquidity

Liquidity is an indication of the business's likely ability to pay its liabilities. Quite simply it is a measure of *do you have enough cash?* The basic measure is liquidity or the *current ratio*, which divides current assets by *current liabilities*:

$$\frac{\text{Current assets (debtors, stocks and cash)}}{\text{Current liabilities (trade creditors, VAT, PAYE, overdraft)}}$$

In simple terms you would expect that a ratio of more than 1 would indicate financial stability, and a ratio of significantly less than 1 would indicate problems. Whilst this is generally a safe working hypothesis, you must compare the ratio calculated against that of other businesses in the same industry ('bench-marking') as, in some sectors, an apparent low liquidity is normal. As for all the ratios covered in this chapter, the following are what you need to know for any figures you calculate:

• Whether, for the industry you are in, the ratio is *relatively* good or bad.

• What the *trend* is over time (increasing or decreasing liquidity).

To generate cash at a known value, stock must first be sold. Stock is, therefore, less 'liquid' than debtors and cash and is also, therefore, less reliable for meeting existing liabilities than are these assets.

The acid test measure of liquidation, therefore, excludes stock to see how readily the business can pay its immediate liabilities:

$$\frac{\text{Debtors and cash}}{\text{Current liabilities}}$$

Gearing

Gearing measures how financially exposed you are. It looks at the extent to which your business's long-term finance is based on borrowed money rather than your funds or 'equity':

$$\frac{\text{Long-term loans}}{\text{Total capital employed}}$$

Again, the importance of the figures lies less in the absolute number and more in how your business compares to other businesses in the sector and long-term trends.

As interest charges on long-term loans will need to be paid whatever the profits generated by the business, the higher the gearing (i.e. the greater the proportion of the business's long-term funding that is borrowed money), the higher will be the business's 'financial' risk.

Example
Company M must pay £20,000 per annum or default on its loan, whilst Company N only has to find £10,000 per annum out of its profits:

	Company M **£000**	**Company N** **£000**
Long-term loans	100	200
Capital	200	100
	300	300
Gearing (%)	33.3 %	66.7 %
Interest cost @ 10% p.a.	10	20

A related measure is interest coverage which shows the sensitivity of available profit in covering interest payments (e.g. to the bank):

$$\frac{\text{Profit before interest}}{\text{Interest}}$$

USING FINANCIAL INFORMATION

Profit centres

To see what is happening to a business it is often helpful to break its performance down into individual areas – at least at the gross profit and contribution level (even if it is impractical to allocate overheads separately).

Example
Company O is an advertising agency that designs adverts, books space for clients and prints brochures. Its monthly management

accounts are as follows:

	£000
Sales	♦
Media	60
Printing	50
Design charges	5
	115
Cost of sales	
Press charges	51
Printers	30
Studio wages	4
Studio direct costs	4
	89
Gross profit	26
Gross profit (%)	22.6%

By breaking this down into different areas of activity ('profit centres'), however, a clearer picture emerges of where Company O does (and does not) make a profit:

	Media	Print	Studio
Sales	60	50	5
Cost of sales	(51)	(30)	(8)
Gross profit/(loss)	9	20	(3)
Gross profit (%)	15	40	(60)

Controlling and analysing costs and trends

A good management technique to ensure that overheads are tightly controlled is 'zero-based budgeting' where, rather than simply taking last year's costs and adding $x\%$ for inflation, you start with a blank sheet of paper and forecast each business cost on a line-by-line basis. Doing this exercise is a good way of ensuring that the requirements for all costs are questioned at least once a year!

Of course, in practice, the requirement to incur most overheads will stay the same year in year out, in which case 'horizontal' and 'vertical' analysis can be used to spot the trends in expenditure.

Example

		Company P				
	Year 1 £000	Year 2 £000	Year 3 £000	Horizontal analysis – Year 1 = 100%		
Sales	100	110	120	100	110	120
Cost of sales	50	60	70	100	120	140
Gross profit	50	50	50	100	100	100
Selling overheads	20	25	25	100	125	125
General overheads	10	12	15	100	120	150
Admin overheads	5	5	6	100	100	120
Net profit	15	8	4	100	53	27

	Vertical analysis – Sales = 100%		
Sales	100	100	100
Cost of sales	50	55	58
Gross profit	50	45	42
Selling overheads	20	23	21
General overheads	10	11	13
Admin overheads	5	5	5
Net profit	15	7	3

Horizontal analysis shows how revenues and costs are growing over time (but be careful to adjust for inflation effects over longer periods). Vertical analysis shows how much of sales each category of expenditure is consuming in each year. You would want to know why general expenses have grown by 50% in three years but, as this is only 13% of sales, the more immediate issue is the increase of cost of sales to 58% of sales (from 50%).

Using cost information

By dividing costs by sales (or by staff number or assets), a pyramid of ratios can be produced which allows you to 'drill down' to look at a business's operating efficiencies. It is most effective when there is good benchmarking data against which to compare the ratios.

Example
Company Q reviews its marketing and finds that 10% of its sales are recycled into TV ads.

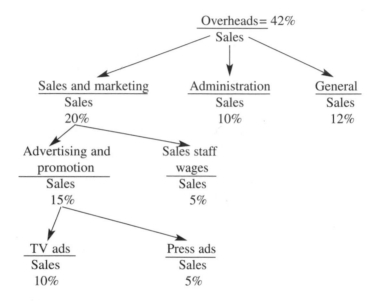

However, by benchmarking, the company finds its competition is spending 20% of sales on TV ads and growing at three times the rate, so perhaps Company Q needs to rethink its promotion strategy.

Management decisions

Use accounting information to assist in decision-making.

Example
Company R currently spends £10,000 on advertising and attracts 100 new customers a year. It is offered an e-business banner advertising package for £5,000 which will be seen by 25,000

people of whom it estimates 10% will be interested and, of these, 1% will become customers. Company R uses costing information to quantify the relative returns and rejects the offer:

	Spend	**New customers**	**Cost per new customer**
Existing	£10,000	100	£100
Package offered	£5,000	25	£200

Management accounts

Companies S, T and U all have identical results for the first quarter and identical year end targets of £1.8m turnover and a profit of £480,000. Company S produces no management accounts (the 'we know how we are doing' mentality). Company T produces a normal, accurate and timely set of accounts.

Company T		
	Month 3 (£000)	**Profit and loss Year to date**
Turnover	100	325
Cost of sales	(40)	(130)
Gross profit	60	195
Gross profit (%)	60	60
Overheads	(50)	(150)
Profit	10	45

Company T's results tell management how they have done so far. But they do not really help Company T's directors to manage the business going forwards.

Company U produces a fuller pack of monthly information in two reports:

Company U: report 1 (£000) – Month 3 profit and loss

	month	Budget	Variance	Explanation
Turnover	100	150	(50)	Widget sales poor due to competitor V's promotion
Cost of sales	(40)	(60)	20	
Gross profit	60	90	(30)	
Gross profit (%)	60	60	60	
Overheads	(50)	(50)	–	
Profit	10	40	(30)	

Company U: Report 2 (£000) – month 3 rolling forecast

	Actual to end month 3	Qtr 2	Qtr 3	Qtr 4	Total	Target
Turnover	325	400	500	700	1,925	1,800
Cost of sales	(130)	(160)	(200)	(280)	(770)	(720)
Gross profit	195	240	300	420	1,155	1,080
Gross profit (%)	60	60	60	60	60	60
Overheads	(150)	(200)	(175)	(150)	675	(600)
Profit	45	40	125	270	480	480

Note: The forecast has been adjusted to show an extra spend of £50K and £25K on promotion in quarters 2 and 3 to drive up sales so as to get back on target.

Company U's monthly management information helps the directors to manage their business because:

- the profit and loss report includes a variance analysis which identifies *quantified differences* between actual and planned performance that require investigation; and

- the monthly revision of a rolling forecast enables the directors to *use the information on current performance to look forward* and to plan the steps that need to be taken to continue to manage performance towards the target for the year (e.g. increasing promotional spending to drive up turnover).

Which company, in your opinion, is helped most in achieving its profit target for the year as a result of its management accounts?

Monitoring return

Investing the company's money in different activities will produce different rates of return.

Example
Company V has a manufacturing arm that makes widgets for sale to third parties, a fitting and servicing arm, and also a repair division, each of which makes a net profit of 10%. From the sale of a fourth business, it now has £100K to invest and needs to decide which activity to develop. How should it decide? One clue lies in looking at the relative returns generated by the investment in assets for each of the businesses (£000):

	Manufacturing and servicing	Fitting	Repair
Assets employee			
Land & buildings	150	25	50
Plant & machinery	50	10	25
Stock	100	5	100
Debtors	150	30	20
Total assets employed	400	70	195
Sales	900	360	50
Profit	90	36	5
Return on assets employed	22.5%	51.4%	2.5%

On the basis of performance to date, an investment in developing the fitting and servicing business may generate over twice the return of investing in the manufacturing business.

What do you think Company V's management should do with the repair arm? Depending on how important the repair facility is to the overall recipe, one answer is that it should be sold and the money realised ploughed into the other two areas. However, before shutting down any operation you need to look carefully at the question of overheads.

Example
Company W has the same areas of business as Company V but its repair arm is making a net loss (£000):

	Manufacturing	Fitting and servicing	Repair	Total
Sales	200	100	50	350
Cost of sales	(100)	(50)	(30)	(180)
Gross profit	100	50	20	170
Overheads	(75)	(40)	(35)	(150)
Profit	25	10	(15)	20

The directors decide to shut the repair arm. Unfortunately, it turned out that they were still left with £20K of the overheads as these related to the premises from which manufacturing and fitting operated, and which now have to bear this cost in full (£000):

	Manufacturing	Fitting and servicing	Total
Sales	200	100	300
Cost of sales	(100)	(50)	(150)
Gross profit	100	50	150
Overheads	(85)	(50)	(135)
Profit	15	—	15

Company W's profit has actually dropped by £5K as a result of shutting down an apparently loss-making operation! This is because the contribution lost was greater than the overheads saved.

Monitoring the working capital cycle

Your accountant may mention 'debtor' or 'creditor days'. The importance of the concept of the 'working capital cycle' to these is set out in Chapter 6. The calculation formulae for these are as follows (in each case take an average value for the asset/liability concerned):

$$\frac{\text{Stock} \times 365}{\text{Purchases}}$$ shows how long it is taking to 'turn over' stock

$$\frac{\text{Creditors} \times 365}{\text{Purchases}}$$ shows how long on average you are taking to pay your suppliers

$$\frac{\text{Debtors} \times 365}{\text{Purchases}}$$ shows how long customers are taking on average to pay their bills

You should always monitor your aged creditor and debtor lists which will reflect these 'days', and you should tie your credit control procedures into your working cashflow forecast.

THE MANAGEMENT/FINANCIAL INFORMATION YOU NEED

To be useful, management information should be gathered *regularly* – prepare it on a regular basis (e.g. weekly/monthly). As far as possible, prepare the information on a *consistent* basis and present it in a consistent way for ease of comparison and for trend spotting. Monthly management accounts should be ready on a *timely* basis by at least week two or three of the following month. Any longer and the accounts are simply history lessons, not management tools. For use in making management decisions, the information needs to be *accurate* (or accurate enough that the difference does not matter).

The information should be *understandable* – clearly laid out, assumptions clearly stated, key points easily identifiable. Wherever possible keep the key points to one or two pages of summary figures (with the rest available for drilling down as required). Many people are uncomfortable when faced with sheets of numbers so, if practical and helpful, use graphs as an alternative way of displaying information (graphs are particularly good for showing trends). Make sure the information is *circulated* – the relevant people need to see the relevant information if it is to be of any use. Finally, the information should be *used* – it should be actively employed to manage the business.

In a particular month, a financial information pack for a business might comprise:

- the profit and loss (including variance analysis – see above);

- the month-end balance sheet;

- aged debtors and creditors; and

- the rolled forward profit and loss (see above) and cashflow forecasts.

But financial information is only part of the story. Your management information should also tell you the key facts on sales (actions, prospects, sales visits planned; performance, average and value, broken down by product, customer/product values, order pipeline, conversion rate per sales visit) and operations (utilisation and efficiency, stock-outs, and customer satisfaction).

SETTING FINANCIAL TARGETS

Your finances provide a reasonable objective measure of your business's performance for comparison between one period and another. Setting realistic but challenging financial performance targets to be met by specific dates is therefore a vital part of putting in place meaningful turnaround objectives for the business.

These can relate to both profit and loss and balance sheet items. For example:

- Achieve turnover growth of 30% p.a. (probably the maximum normally sustainable level of growth for most businesses).

- Bank borrowings at a level with which the bank will feel secure (say 45% of debtors less than three months and 20% of fixed assets).

SETTING FINANCIAL TARGETS FOR YOUR BUSINESS

Decide how would you define a 'stabilised situation' for your business (e.g. creditor payments might be on normal trade terms for your business of two months' purchases):

	Stable	**Ideal**
Profitability		
Growth		
Stock position		
Creditor payments		
Bank lending vs security		
Liquidity		
Gearing		

Now quantify what financial targets you would set for your business to hit (£000):

Profit and loss

	Now	3 months	1 year	2 years	5 years
Turnover					
Gross profit					
Gross profit %					
Overheads					
Net profit					

Balance sheet

	Now	3 months	1 year	2 years	5 years
Fixed assets					
Stock					
Debtors					
Cash					
Trade creditors					
PAYE/NI/VAT creditors					
Other finance/ loans					

How quickly can you achieve a stable situation? How quickly can you achieve an ideal situation? What do you need to do to know you are operating your business in such a way so as to achieve these targets?

Now summarise the profit improvement steps you need to take on the following chart.

Profit improvement plan:

Current profit   £

Steps to be taken   *By date*   *Profit effect*

1 _____

2 _____

3 _____

4 _____

5 _____

6 _____

7 _____

8 _____

9 _____

10 _____

Required profit

PART 3

DEVISE A PLAN

There is nothing more difficult to handle, more doubtful of success, and more dangerous to carry through than initiating changes . . . The innovator makes enemies of all those who prospered under the old order, and only lukewarm support is forthcoming from those who would prosper under the new . . . partly from fear . . . and partly because men are generally incredulous, never really trusting new things unless they have tested them by experience.

The Prince, Niccolo Macchiavelli
George Bull translation, Penguin Classics

8

Setting the Strategy

IT'S YOUR BUSINESS: WHAT DO YOU WANT TO DO?

The steps outlined so far will help you to stabilise your business. However, the point of a turnaround is that it should enable you to go on to rebuild your business. In order to be able to do this, you need to put in place a regrowth strategy. The steps involved in creating such a strategy are as follows.

First, think through what you want to achieve personally from the business and *set your personal goals*. Next, understand (as far as possible) the big 'external' forces that affect your industry and business and what *opportunities and threats* arise from these.

- What is happening in the business environment? (Carry out a PEST analysis – see below.)

- What forces are shaping the structure of your industry and how much money can be made from your industry? (See industry structure: 'Porter's five forces' below.)

You must now understand your own business and its *strengths and weaknesses*:

- What products are you supplying into which markets, and what potential growth strategies are there?

- Where are your products in their lifecycles and have you got an appropriate portfolio of products?

- What do your customers want?

- What is your competitive advantage (based on what your customers want) within your industry and on which you can build?

- What is your unique selling proposition?

Finally, decide what strategy to pursue and then create an appropriate value chain and put in place an action plan.

SETTING YOUR PERSONAL GOALS

To set your business strategy you will need a plan that matches:

- your ambitions for your business;

- your type of business; and

- the circumstances you find yourself in.

Rather than being proscriptive, much of this book is set out in the form of structured sets of questions for you to ask yourself about your business which should lead you through a process that will help you to create your own plan. To produce a meaningful set of personal goals it is worth asking yourself three questions.

1. Why are you in business — what motivates you?

Is it:

- The sheer *challenge*, the satisfaction of overcoming obstacles and winning through, or beating the opposition day after day?

- A drive to be *creative*, using your business as a way of making your dreams real?

- *Independence*, in that you need to be free to operate in the way you want to, without being told what to do?

- A sense of *security and stability* where you are looking to feel you have 'made it' and are financially secure?

- A mixture of all the above and, if so, in what proportion?

2. What type of skill have you based your business on?

Is it:

- Your *specific technical expertise*, where you have developed skills as a doer or seller and want to exploit them to the full? (But beware of the administrative burden of running your own small business, which will get worse as the business grows in size.)

- Your *general management skills*, where it's not your own specialism but your ability to manage other people that provides the basis for the business?

3. What are you trying to achieve by being in business?

Is it:

- A *comfortable lifestyle* with a good short- or long-term balance of work and outside interests?

- To *building up* or *maintaining a stable business* to hand on to the next generation?

- To *build a business for sale* to allow you to go on to other projects?

- To *expand your business* to be the biggest or best in the industry?

- To act as a *provider of some special service or value*, perhaps expressing some deeply held religious or other values (such as environmentalism), and perhaps even run deliberately as a non-profit-making organisation?

Having a clear view of what motivates you, of what types of skills you have based your business on and of what you are trying to achieve in running your business is critical to setting meaningful goals.

Having established your personal goals, you will want to run your business to achieve these. You then need to turn these goals into a set of objectives that are SMART:

Specific.
Measurable – that can quantify the results.
Achievable.
Relevant.
Time bounded – are governed by deadlines.

This will allow you to specify the actions you will need to take in managing your business to achieve these goals and to start to prioritise your goals using the ease/impact matrix from Chapter 6 (Figure 13). So think through what it is you are trying to achieve and then fill out a table like the one shown in Figure 17.

Has this helped you to clarify what you are trying to do and the things you need to make happen to achieve this? Having undertaken this exercise you should also ask yourself the following questions:

- What are my key managers'/staff's personal goals?

- Are these compatible with my goals and my business strategy?

If there are major differences (Fred, in production, wants the quiet life, but your strategy calls for a significant expansion of the business), you now have an early warning of a likely management issue. This will give you the direction you want to

Goals	Measures	Timescale for achieving	Actions	Importance	Ease
What is important to me? What am I trying to achieve from running this business?	How will I know I have achieved this? What does it look/feel like?	How long will it take?	What do I need to do to make this happen?	How important is this to me? Rank on scale 0–10	How easy will it be to take the action? Rank on scale 0–10
Financial security	*Mortgage paid off*	*5 years*	*Build company to profit £100K p.a.*	9	5
	Pension fund of £100K by the time I am 55	*10 years*	*Sell company*		
More free time	*Home every Sunday*	*1 year*	*Bring in salesperson*	7	8
	Able to take holiday	*1 year*	*Delegate administration*		

Fig. 17. A personal goals summary.

go in. However, there will be factors outside your control that will be influencing your business and that you will need to analyse.

INDUSTRIAL TRENDS: 'PEST' ANALYSIS

The world is a changing place. Developments across a range of factors will have an impact on your industry or business. So, ask yourself: What are the major trends in the business environment in which I am operating that will affect my industry and business?

There are four main headings you need to consider for any industry (PEST analysis), so complete a table like the one shown in Figure 18 for your business.

Politics/legislation	• *Requirement for all widget users to be licensed from next year* • *EU widget standard announced* • *Privatisation of French state-owned widget manufacturer*
Economics	• *Coming out of recession, long-term growth expected* • *Widget raw material prices will rise* • *Growth of industrial widget users slowing* • *Direct selling of widgets taking off*
Social	• *Demand for recyclable widgets* • *Domestic widgets becoming fashionable*
Technological	• *Digital widgets to become commercially viable within two years*

Fig. 18. PEST analysis.

Perhaps a fifth heading should be added to these: *industry realignment*, e.g. European and US widget makers entering the UK market and purchasing small UK manufacturers. How is the impact of these factors going to change your industry over the next five years? How does your business need to change to meet any threats arising (e.g. a need to invest) or opportunities opening up (eg new markets or an opportunity to sell the business)?

INDUSTRY STRUCTURE: 'PORTER'S FIVE FORCES'

The attractiveness of any industry and the potential to make significant profits tend to be governed by the interaction of a number of forces. These can be analysed by asking the five key questions shown in Figure 19.

WHAT PRODUCTS TO SELL INTO WHICH MARKETS?

Most business will have a 'portfolio' of products and markets. The starting point for assessing your opportunities to sell particular products in particular markets is by way of a product/market ('Ansoff') matrix (see Figure 20).

Set out a basic matrix for your business by asking the two questions shown in the figure.

Once you have plotted this, do some more homework:

- What is the *size* of each product market box (*segment*) as a potential market?

- How much do you sell into this box (your *'share'*)?

- Is the market demand in that segment *growing, steady* or *declining*?

The four basic growth strategies for any business are then (in normal order of ease/risk) as follows.

1. Market penetration

Improve your market penetration *by boosting sales to your existing customers who already know you and your products:*

- Look for the *gaps* – UK supermarkets (existing customers) are not taking any widgets (an existing product). Why not? What can you do to change this?
- Increase your *share of a channel* – do you supply 1%, 10% or

What will keep other people out of your industry (barriers to entry)?

The requirements for:

- regulation/licensing
- high investment in capital/brand building
- high economy of scale/learning curves
- restricted access to distribution channels or technology

will mean it is difficult for newcomers to enter the industry and to threaten prices (e.g. how easy is it to set up a new airline?)

How intense is competition within the industry?

The existence of:

- high 'exit' barriers
- a lack of a differentiated product
- high fixed costs
- industry overcapacity

will imply intense competition and price pressure (e.g. how high are margins in the petrol refining part of the industry?)

What substitute products are there?

The existence of:

- high rates of legislation or technological change
- low switching costs for consumers
- high savings from new products
- fashion changes

will mean new alternative products can rapidly replace existing suppliers (e.g. how secure in the long term is any computer software or hardware business?)

Who has more power, you or your customer?

Do the following conditions apply?

- a few buyers and many sellers
- commodity products
- the buyer controls distribution channels
- the buyer has low switching costs between suppliers.

These mean the customer will tend to have the whip hand (e.g. who has the power, supermarkets or most of their suppliers?)

Who has more power, you or your supplier?

Do the following conditions apply?

- few suppliers and many buyers
- differentiated products
- no satisfactory substitute.

These mean the supplier's negotiating power is high (e.g. Heinz ketchup)

Fig. 19. Porter's five forces.

What products do you supply?	What markets/customer group distribution channels do you supply?			
	Direct to the public by mail order	Small UK shops	UK supermarkets	*New channel*
Widgets	√	√	–	X
Thingamies	√	√	√	
Servicing	–	√	√	
New product	Y			Z

Fig. 20. A product/market ('Ansoff') matrix.

100% of small UK shops' demand for widgets? How can you increase your share of that customer/market's spend on this type of product?

As these customers already know you, try holding a regular service review meeting (or quality control review) to create opportunities to ask for more business. Send them a newsletter, a loyalty discount and new product details.

2. New customers and markets

Develop new customers and *markets* for your existing products (e.g. for widgets, box X):

• Can you persuade existing customers to refer new customers to you by incentivising them?

• Can you identify new types or groups of customers to whom you can sell (e.g. the company in Figure 20 might think about approaching garage chains or overseas distributors).

3. New products

Develop new products based on your existing core skills to sell to your existing customers to meet their other needs (i.e. box Y). How about the company in Figure 20 adding on a widget rental business, or becoming the UK licensee of the new Italian 'Gadgetti'?

4. Diversification

Finally, and most risky of all, there is diversification (i.e. box Z) – developing a new product for supply to a new set of customers. This is risky because you need to develop a new product about which you have no knowledge and sell it into a new market where you have little existing credibility as potential customers do not know you. So even if you do decide to diversify, try to make it a logical step based on some of your core skills or strengths so as to minimise your risk.

To achieve most from each of the above strategies, you will need to focus on the most attractive product/market segments, which are those:

- *with high growth*;

- *where you make high profits* (can you analyse your profit and loss by product/market segment to give you this information – see Chapter 7); and

- *where you have the most strength on which to grow.*

PRODUCT LIFECYCLES AND PRODUCT PORTFOLIOS

Products have lifecycles (they either eventually fade away, are overtaken by newer products or have to be reinvented). This process can take many years (the ocean liner) or may be extremely fast (this year's fashion) – see Figure 21.

New products tend to eat cash in their development and marketing stages as they try to increase their market share. It is only when they become established that they generate surplus cash.

The Boston Consulting Group matrix (Figure 22) is used when analysing a portfolio of products or businesses (where new products start out as 'question marks').

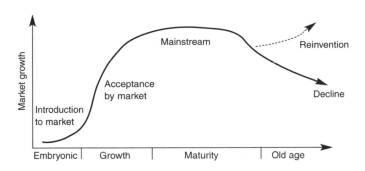

Fig. 21. The product lifecycle.

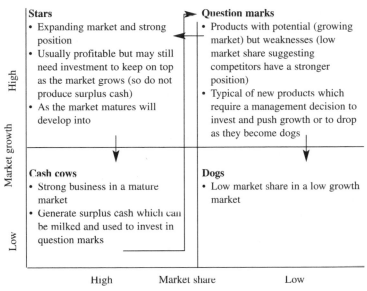

Fig. 22. The Boston Consulting Group matrix.

MEETING CUSTOMER EXPECTATIONS (THE CRITICAL SUCCESS FACTORS)

Take a step back for a moment and ask yourself or, even better, ask your customers, what is important to them in making their decisions about whom to buy from:

- What are the things all potential suppliers must have been able to do to be considered? (*Order qualifiers* – which airline will fly me from Heathrow to New York?)

- What are the things that decide which of the potential suppliers is actually chosen? (*Order winners* – which airline will offer the best seats, food and frequent flier programme?)

Rank the importance of these factors on a scale of 0 to 10 (as in the example in Figure 23), together with how you think (or, better, your customers tell you) your own performance and that of your competitors rate.

Critical factors	Importance to customers	Our performance	Competitor A
Price	6	7	3
Quality	9	6	10
Range	4	10	5
Service backup	8	9	10
Speed of delivery	3	5	1

Fig. 23. Critical performance factors.

Take another step back and ask yourself why these factors are important to your customers. What need are customers satisfying in buying from you? Why do they want to buy your product at all? This is important as customers purchase to achieve *benefits* (i.e. the ability to have a hole when they need one) rather than *features* (this drill is made of high-speed steel). So you will need to focus your marketing on addressing how customers' *needs* are met by your service (which are often emotional), *not* on its *features* (which are often technical). You then need to graph your performance (see Figure 24).

If you are competing against competitor A for an order, you

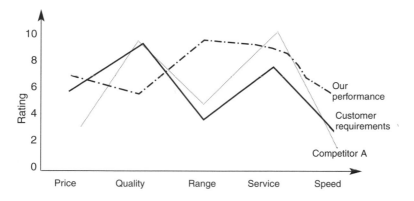

Fig. 24. Graphing critical performance factors.

can immediately see, for example, that you should be stressing your better price performance (where A is a long way below the customer's ideal requirement).

In the longer term, however, you can also see that you are significantly over-delivering in the area of range of products carried (which customers do not value highly) and under-delivering in the area of quality (which they do). This suggests the range of products produced should be reduced to focus on higher quality products.

COMPETITIVE ADVANTAGE

Long-term success relies on establishing and maintaining a 'competitive advantage' over your present and future competitors. It's not rocket science but I use a simple formula that summarises the key points that you need to manage. Competitive advantage (A) can be summarised as:

$$A = \frac{(B, C, D) \times W^k - X}{£N}$$

©TM

This means having a successful recipe for doing things better (B), cheaper (C) or differently (D) from your competitors in a way customers want and know about (W^K), which competitors cannot copy (X - for Xerox), and which overall makes money now (£N). You then need to keep it successful (so it remains based on what customers want and is not copied). The best way to do this is to use a chart such as the one shown in Figure 25.

What do we do that is?	How do we do it?	Why does this matter to our customers?	Can this be copied?
Better in a way that customers can identify and perceive as delivering extra value			
Cheaper for us to do than for our competitors	Through better innovation, automation and waste management we can manufacture at 25% less than our competitors	We can sell cheaper than our competitors	Partly; would require major investment in machinery but it would be difficult to replicate our know-how
Different that specifically meets the needs of particular groups of customers	We make the only left-handed widget	Left-handed people find right-handed widgets very awkward	Yes, but it's a small market and probably not worth anyone else investing in the machinery

Fig. 25. Maintaining competitive advantage.

You can work at creating and maintaining competitive advantage by focusing on developing your business's strengths in a variety of areas. The key areas to develop are as follows:

- *Reputation* - for many products (e.g. from brain surgery to motor oil) it is often very difficult to inspect the quality of the goods prior to purchase, so many customers will rely on brand names and reputation as a 'safe choice', even if this means paying a premium.

- *Strategic assets* - where investing in gaining dominance in a narrow niche (e.g. left-handed widgets) or in capital equipment, economies of scale, sewing up the key suppliers or distribution networks, know-how and improved skills from learning curve effects or in creating an industry standard (e.g. Microsoft Windows) can give you a significant advantage over competitors.

- The ability both successfully and commercially to *innovate* and develop new and better ways of doing things or products and services can give you an advantage over your competitors (but you also need to manage the risks associated with innovation).

- *Internal organisation and infrastructure* (such as efficient stock and wastage control or internal communication) will make you more efficient than your competitors.

- *External networks* can also help, such as joint ventures and strategic alliances or membership of a purchasing ring.

UNIQUE SELLING PROPOSITIONS

To stand out from your competitors, you are going to need to communicate what is different about your business's products and services from those of your competitors. This is known as your 'unique selling proposition' (USP).

You should already have a good idea of what your USP is, so try the following experiment:

1. List all the words you could use to describe what is really different in the eyes of your customers about your business and that distinguish it from your competition.

2. Now cross out all those which your *competitors* would use. If you and your competitors would both use these words, customers are not getting a message you are different. (And if you are not different, why buy from you?)

3. What words do you have left?

4. What do these words tell you about how you should structure

your advertising and promotion, and what do they imply about your potential market? For example, if the only word left on your list is 'local', then the potential market for your current operation is restricted to the local area unless you can:

- come up with another distinguishing USP with a wider application; or

- increase your number of places of sale (see Chapter 9) to have more 'local' markets.

5. Now, put together a short sentence (preferably three to five words) that summarises not just who you are but that also explains to your customers why they should buy from you. For the company, we have been looking at here, it is 'The lowest cost widget'. As a company rescue expert, for my business it is 'I save businesses'. From now on, make this sentence your motto: the rationale for everything you do, your mission in life. Yes, this sentence is a real mission statement. *Your mission is to bring that promise to your customers*.

THE VALUE CHAIN

Once you have your 'motto' (or mission), you need to make your business and all your employees live it in every aspect of your operations to make it *real*. In other words, to ensure that you deliver exactly what the customer wants, you must ensure that all aspects of your business are consistently focused on your mission, which is to supply what the customers want (see Figure 26).

FAMILY BUSINESSES

While family businesses tend to have particular strengths in terms of commitment and family members' long schooling in the business's culture and operation, they also have a specific need that must be considered when setting strategy – the interaction between the family and the business. When a decision has to be taken, in whose interest is it made: the family's, or in the interests of the business?

The specific issues family businesses need to address are as follows.

Succession

Restricting the opportunity of becoming senior managers or directors to family members only can be a huge drawback on the potential talent available to the business.

External capital

A similar drawback is a reluctance to allow 'outsiders' to participate in the company's equity.

External skills

It is often difficult to attract high quality external management into a family business as such people will be conscious that the centre of power lies within the family structures (i.e. decisions are taken around the Sunday dinner table rather than through formal business structures). There may also be limits to promotion, where certain roles are reserved for family members only.

Investment

Some family businesses invest in or carry on with parts of the business on the basis of tradition ('grandfather started the business making widgets so we cannot stop now') rather than commercial logic.

Fairness

If family members are employed in the business, how fair is their treatment in comparison to non-family employees (e.g. on timekeeping), and what effect does this special treatment have on staff morale?

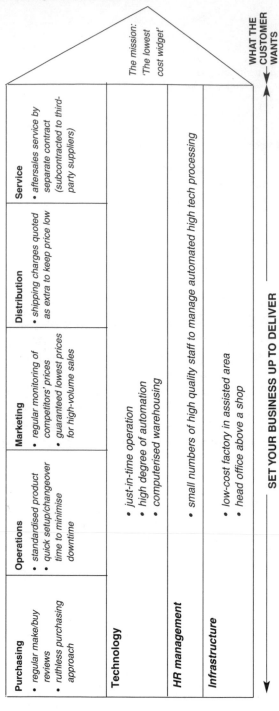

Fig. 26. The value chain.

Purchasing	Operations	Marketing	Distribution	Service	
• regular make/buy reviews • ruthless purchasing approach	• standardised product • quick setup/changeover time to minimise downtime	• regular monitoring of competitors' prices • guaranteed lowest prices for high-volume sales	• shipping charges quoted as extra to keep price low	• aftersales service by separate contract (subcontracted to third-party suppliers)	The mission: 'The lowest cost widget'
Technology	• just-in-time operation • high degree of automation • computerised warehousing				
HR management	• small numbers of high quality staff to manage automated high tech processing				
Infrastructure	• low-cost factory in assisted area • head office above a shop				

WHAT THE CUSTOMER WANTS

SET YOUR BUSINESS UP TO DELIVER

Diversion of resources

In a family business that is regarded as 'owned by the family' (or an individual entrepreneur), there can be a risk that company funds are used to meet personal expenditure (e.g. telephone bills, parking tickets, subscriptions, etc.) to the detriment of the business as a whole.

The 'I don't want to be here' syndrome

Occasionally, family members may go into the business because they are 'expected' to do so rather than as a result of any vocation or aptitude for the business.

Dilution of interest

As the firm passes down the generations, shareholding can become subdivided into smaller and smaller lots, which can lead to potential difficulties in obtaining clear decisions about some issues. This can be particularly accentuated when the family shareholders are divided into those who are involved and those who are not involved in the management of the business.

SETTING BUSINESS GOALS AND DECIDING ON AN ACTION PLAN

If you have not already done so, work your way through each of the exercises in this chapter to obtain results for your own business. On the basis of these results, go on to set out your proposed business goals and action plan.

Now check your plan:

- Is it realistic, based on the resources you have available (both cash and people)?

- Are the key staff (and external stakeholders) sufficiently motivated to stay with you to see it through?

- Does your plan balance your short-term needs to generate cash with your long-term business development aims?

Business's name _____

Your's business's motto or mission _____

Business goal What are we/ am I going to do?	Measure What will the measure of success be?	Timescale How long will it take?	Responsibility Who is going to do it?	Action What are they going to do to achieve the goal?	Resources What will they need?	Constraints What may cause them problems?	Solutions How can they get over the difficulty?	Importance Rank on scale of 0 to 10	Ease Rank on scale 0 to 10

- Does it take into account any resistance to change? How are you going to deal with this?

Next, draw up a project timetable. Set out visually what needs to happen so you can monitor progress (see Figure 27).

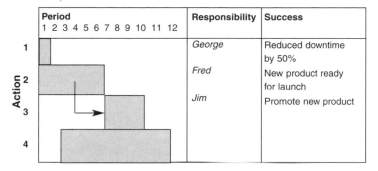

Fig. 27. A project timetable.

Note: Action 3 follows on from completing action 2.

9
Managing Marketing

SUCCESSFUL MARKETING

Successful marketing comes from having both an *attractive offering* and an *effective sales effort*. This is because people will buy a package they believe gives them the right value proposition (the 'offering') comprising the right product, with the right quality/benefits package, at the right price, place and time. They know about the package and it is this knowledge that convinces them to buy ('sales').

Having worked through your strategy, you should be well on your way to having a compelling offering. This chapter, therefore, is about the marketing of that offering and about effective selling.

THE IMPORTANCE OF MARKETING

Small businesses can suffer from some or all of four classic marketing problems:

1. *Failure to put together a clear USP* (unique selling proposition) based on a sustainable competitive advantage and with a value chain to back it up.

2. *Failure to put together a marketing plan*, particularly in a business set up by people who are good at 'doing something'.

3. *A 'feast/famine' sales programme*, when sales effort falls away as people obtain business and where there should be a programme to build an ongoing 'sales machine'.

4. *Poor control of a salesforce.*

To achieve significant growth, your business cannot simply rely on business coming to you. You will have to go out actively to seek it in order to gain market size and share. To do so, you need to draw up a marketing plan covering:

- whom you are going to sell to;
- how you are going to sell, the marketing mix (the four Ps of price, product, promotion, place – and a sales plan); and
- your management of the salesforce.

DECIDING WHOM TO SELL TO

To plan your marketing approach (what you are going to say and where and how you are going to say it), you need to identify whom you are going to sell to. There are many ways to 'segment' your market to identify customer profiles. For consumer markets the four main variables are as follows:

1. *Geographic:*
- region
- climate
- city size.

2. *Psychographic:*
- social class
- lifestyle
- personality.

3. *Demographic:*
- age/gender
- income/occupation
- education.

4. *Behavioural:*
- user (heavy/light, regular/occasional)
- attitude/awareness
- loyalty
- benefits sought (speed, price, quality).

If your market is working-class men in Scotland and you advertise only in glossy women's magazines in Kent, your marketing is poorly targeted. For industrial purchasers, geographic and behavioural segmentation also applies, together with other variables, such as:

- Purchasing approach, degree of centralisation, membership of purchasing ring, price/quality/service focus.

- Attitude to risk.

- Seasonality, urgency, size of order, distress purchase.

In addition to making your selling effort effective, segmentation can enable you to identify new market opportunities by highlighting particular segments into which different products can be sold:

- *Horizontal segmentation* – providing different versions of products that suit the different needs of each segment (from the CL version widget to the GSXI turbo RS competitor special widget).

- *Vertical segmentation* – providing the same product at different prices/levels for each segment.

Example
When buying transaltantic airline tickets, customer preferences for comfort and price cluster into two areas, allowing two classes of services to be offered on the same plane (see Figure 28).

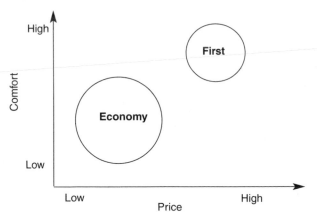

Fig. 28. Customers' preferences for airline tickets.

By identifying and understanding your customers better, you can also tailor your marketing message so it is likely to be more effective.

Customers behave differently depending on how much variety there is on offer and how important choice is to them. This can help you in planning your message to them (see Figure 29).

		Importance of purchase to customer	
		Low	High
Brand differences	Many	*Cakes* Seek variety ——— Needs a wide range of choice	*Cars* Costly purchase, buy infrequently, seen as risky and expressive of image and lifestyle Customers can do a lot of research and often form strong views in advance of purchase ——— Provide lots of information in advance and advertise to project a strong image
	Few	*Butter* Buy out of habit or purchase price ——— Need a lot of advertising to create awareness	*Hi fi* Buy infrequently and can detect little difference between brands ——— Support aftersales to help them stay convinced they have made the right choice

Fig. 29. Customer buying behaviour.

HOW TO SELL YOUR PRODUCT

Your customers do not just buy a 'product'; they are actually buying a whole package of tangible and intangible products and services (see Figure 30).

In order to sell efficiently, you need to:

- tailor your marketing to your customers (using the four Ps of marketing);

- manage the sales process; and

- manage your salesforce.

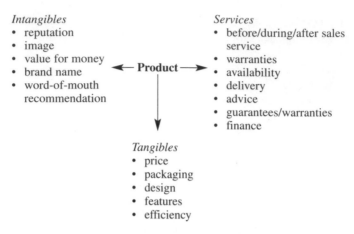

Intangibles
- reputation
- image
- value for money
- brand name
- word-of-mouth recommendation

← **Product** →

Services
- before/during/after sales service
- warranties
- availability
- delivery
- advice
- guarantees/warranties
- finance

Tangibles
- price
- packaging
- design
- features
- efficiency

Fig. 30. The product 'package'.

TAILORING MARKETING STRATEGY: THE FOUR Ps OF MARKETING

There are four main areas under your control where you can make changes to your marketing strategy:

1. *Price:*

- list price
- credit policy
- financing
- incentives
- discount structure.

2. *Product:*

- branding
- product features
- product quality
- packaging
- warranties
- service backup.

3. *Promotion:*

- advertising
- point of sale
- brochures/promotional material
- samples
- salesforce
- mailshots
- telesales.

4. *Place:*

- distribution channels
- geographic coverage
- location of outlets.

Your approach to these is known as your marketing mix. What is your strategy/policy in respect of each of the above points for your product? How does your approach compare to those of your competitors? Is it well suited to your target market? What changes can you make (try a pilot scheme first) which might increase profits through the net effect on sales (e.g. quantity discounts)?

MANAGING THE SALES PROCESS

Small businesses will often suffer from 'feast and famine' marketing where, as work comes in, the effort on marketing ceases, only to pick up again when work dries up. If you suffer from this, you need to work to smooth out this fluctuation by putting a structured sales process in place. To generate sales on a regular basis, you need to have a sales machine in action day in/day out based on the sales funnel principle (see Figure 31).

Example

Fig. 31. The sales funnel.

On a monthly basis:
- 1,000 mailshots produce . . .
- 25 enquiries, which produce . . .
- 10 sales meetings, which produce . . .
- 5 quotes, which produce . . .
- 2 sales.

At an average sales value of, say, £2,500, this funnel leads to £5,000 turnover per month.

This approach allows you not only to have a regular flow of sales but also to manage the process. For example, if you wanted to increase monthly sales by £10,000 to £15,000, you could either:

- send out an extra 2,000 mailshots each month and resource sales staff to follow up 50 more enquiries and attend 20 more sales meetings; or

- look to increase the efficiency of the existing process. For example, if following up mailshots with telephone calls can increase the leads/enquiries from the existing response rate of

2.5% to 7.5%, and the remaining statistics stay the same, you can achieve the required increase with no increase in mailshots.

MANAGING THE SALESFORCE

If you have a salesforce, you must ensure you make the best use of it. Use the following checklist to help you.

Given the market segmentation you are looking to supply to, what is the best way to organise your selling effort? Is it by geographical area, product or market? Is this how you are currently organised?	
What is your business's selling style (harder sell focused on one-off sales, or softer sell, based on longer-term relationships)? Is it appropriate for your products and markets?	
Have your sales staff got the appropriate personality types for your preferred approach?	
Have you got the right numbers of sales people?	
What do the customers need from the salesforce – information, aftersales support, training? How effectively do you meet those needs?	
Are there customer needs you could meet more cost effectively by other means?	
How do customers rate your customer service?	
How do you pay your sales staff (fixed salary, commission, etc.)? Is the pay structure efficient to motivate them to achieve your marketing objectives?	
How does the pay compare with competitors?	
How good is your sales manager at motivating and coaching the salesforce?	

Does the salesforce feel comfortable with the quality and value delivered by the company once the sale is made?	
Is your sales staff turnover better or worse than the industry average?	
Why do you lose good sales staff?	
What promotion prospects/career paths can you offer good sales staff?	
How do you manage sales staff performance? Is the basis of measurement both relevant and clearly understood by the sales staff?	
What targets does the salesforce have?	
Are they involved in producing these or are they imposed 'top down'?	
Do targets relate to the expected relative values of different sales territories?	
Are the targets both performance ratios and absolute measures?	
Do the targets tie in to the pay structure (e.g. stepped commission)?	
What happens to under, or significant over, performances?	
Are your sales staff trained (on or off the job, e.g. at sales meetings) in both the product and in selling techniques? (For example, how to set out the product's benefits not its features, how to ask for the business and how to close a sale.)	
How fast do you respond to customer enquiries?	
How good are delivery times?	
How well are complaints handled? Is your paperwork efficiently produced and user-friendly?	

KEY POINTS

* Work out your personal goals.

* Use the following formula for business success (after Duggan, Porter and Kay) to set your strategy:

$$A = \frac{(B, C, D) \times W^K - X}{£N} \text{ ©TM}$$

(Doing something **B**etter, **C**heaper, and/or **D**ifferently)

x

that customers **W**ant and ᴷnow about

—

Long-term competitive = **A**dvantage	that cannot be **X**eroxed by your competitors
	that, overall, makes money (**£**) **N**ow ©TM

* Build your business to deliver this formula.

* Keep refreshing it.

* Manage your marketing and sales effort to make your customers aware of your excellent offering.

10

Managing Change

To 'make it happen' in your business you have to:

- *Manage and motivate yourself.* You are the key resource in your business and, if you don't make it happen, no one else will.

- *Understand your business's structure, culture and staff* – as they exist now and how you want them to be in the future.

- *Manage people and the process of change*, using techniques to make change happen as efficiently as possible.

- *Get stakeholders on board and keep them there* throughout the planned change.

MANAGING AND MOTIVATING YOURSELF

In your business, you are *the* key resource. You therefore need to manage yourself very carefully to ensure you use yourself as efficiently and effectively as possible. The key areas to address, and some business approaches appropriate to those areas, are as follows.

Self-motivation and time management

Visualisation
Take your list of goals. Make a collage of pictures illustrating each measure of success (that fast car, the golf clubs, the family, the pile of money, the holiday). Hang it in your office where you see it every day.

Make it real
Commit yourself to achieving some small short-term goal by paying the deposit for the holiday in six months. As you achieve your goals, put a big red tick on the picture!

Measure
For the next two weeks, record for each 15 minutes what you have done. Put a cost on your time. How much has each activity *cost* you? What was useful and you should do more of? What was a waste of time and you should drop? What could be done more cost effectively or by someone else?

Prioritise
Take 10 minutes at the end of each day to plan the next day's work. List all the tasks you want to achieve and group them by priority:

- Urgent and important (do).

- Urgent but not important (do, but don't waste time on).

- Important but not urgent (make sure they are done before they become urgent).

- Not important or urgent (delegate).

Your 'important' priorities ought to tie into your overall objectives and goals. If you are carrying tasks forward day after day, this means:

- they are not important and you should be delegating them to someone else;

- your time is overloaded (and you need to delegate); and

- it's a task you do not want to face up to/find time for (if so, what are you going to do about it?).

Be assertive
When you want things done try using the three part
assertiveness mantra:

- What I like is . . .

- What I don't like is . . .

- What I want is . . .

UNDERSTANDING YOUR BUSINESS'S STRUCTURE AND CULTURE

Some of the strongest forces operating within your business are
its culture and structure but, because they have often grown up
over time, they have never been formally set out. They form a
pervasive background but this 'wood' is often all but invisible to
those working inside the business who see only the trees.

Your business's culture and structure are different but linked.
The *culture* of your business is the shared *values, experience*
and *beliefs* of the business that set out 'how we do things here':

- independently of management;

- informally; and

- including war stories, in-jokes, reputations, myths, etc.

The *structure* of your business is how it is organised:

- as set out by management;

- formally; and

- as perceived by the public (e.g. through organisation charts).

As businesses develop in size and complexity, cultural style and
structure often develop along parallel lines from a power to a
role culture and from an entrepreneurial to a functional structure
(see Figures 32 and 33).

Culture styles	Structure types
Power Overall leader makes all the decisions	*Entrepreneurial* Owner manager in direct contact with all staff
Role Job specifications exist and staff are expected to fulfil their responsibilities	*Functional* Structured command with defined hierarchy and lines of control

Fig. 32. Culture styles and structure types.

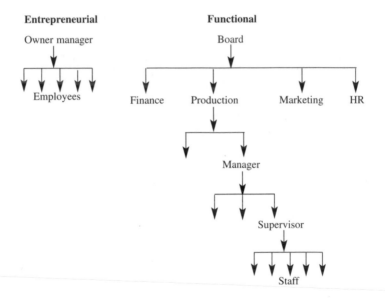

Fig. 33. Entrepreneurial and functional structures.

To help you to manage your people and business through a process of change, take a step back from your own business:

- *Draw an organisation chart showing who formally reports to whom.* How clearly structured is it? How logically organised is it?

- Take a different coloured pen and mark on your plan the *lines of power* – who goes to whom for decisions. Does this follow the 'formal structure'? If not, why not? (For example, Fred is the factory manager, but all the lads on the shopfloor still come to you as 'the boss' for all the decisions.)

- Put a *job title* by everyone on your chart. Do they make sense given the lines you have drawn?

- For each of the *key roles* in your business, is someone shown as being clearly responsible for these?

There are two further business culture/structure pairings (see Figures 34 and 35).

Culture styles	Structure types
Task The focus is on completing a specific task rather than on performing a business function	*Matrix* Teams assembled to operate on a project basis as required (e.g. consultancy firms or large engineering projects)
Resource Individuals' requirements take priority over those of the organisation	*Specialist* Professional practice (e.g. barristers), where individuals practise with common support mechanisms

Fig. 34. Specialised culture styles and structure types.

These pairings tend to evolve in specialised circumstances. For example, in a major engineering operation, each client project may have a manager (A, B or C) whose job it is to manage the project on behalf of the customer by purchasing services from the business's various departments, such as production, HR, etc.

ASSESSING YOUR TEAM

Who is in charge of sales, marketing, customer services, purchasing, production, despatch, quality control, research and development, finance, personnel, overall strategic direction and drive? (If this last isn't you, who is it and why?)

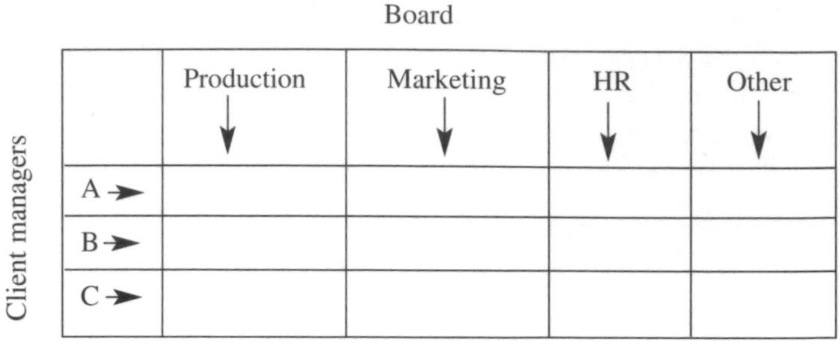

Board

	Production	Marketing	HR	Other
A ➤				
B ➤				
C ➤				

Client managers

Fig. 35. A matrix structure.

Assess your team by completing the checklist shown in Figure 36 for each of the above roles. Once you have done so, do you have any gaps? Do you have roles filled but where your assessment indicates a potential problem (e.g. George is unqualified, unwilling to change, lacks commitment and has an inappropriate personality)? How crucial are any gaps to achieving your plan? (For example, how are you going to manage your growth plan with no one in charge of IT and with George dealing with the financing issues?)

If this exercise has identified a personnel issue, are you missing one of the following:

1) A necessary *functional role* (e.g. a financial director or a quality controller)? If this is the case, can you cover the role yourself? Do you need to recruit (and is this a full-time or part-time post)? Or is it a temporary need (could you use an interim manager)?

2) A temporary *situational skill* where, if you don't have someone in-house who can do it, you need to get someone in who can? Help with situational skills comes from *doers* (interim managers or company doctors appointed to take responsibility for doing a particular task) or *advisers* (consultants, mentors, coaches or professional advisers – e.g. accountants or insolvency practitioners – who are hired to help you do what is needed by advising on the steps you need to take).

Person	Role	Qualification	Experience and industry knowledge	Ability to think strategically	Financial awareness	Team type	Personality type	Record of delivery	Experience of bad times?	Willingness to change	Commitment to company and plan/interest in outcome
Fred	Production manager	Engineering degree	7 years with Widget Inc as line manager	Limited, very much a 'nuts and bolts' man, internally focused	Focused on cost management. Can read a P&L	Driver, comes up with a plan and ensures it is seen through. Good evaluator and completer-finisher	Goal orientated, practical. Reserved with people, works in a structured way	Strong within own sphere	Yes, 2 year slump at Widget Inc.	Will change once works through for himself that change is needed	Appears loyal and strongly committed
George	Accountant	'By experience'	Company accountant and bookkeeper since 1956	A bookkeeper's bookkeeper	None, a number cruncher, not a manager	Solitary worker	Jobsworth. Poor communicator. No imagination	Produces numbers but unable to help manage finances	None	Dislikes change	Retiring in 2 years

Fig. 36. Management assessment: checklist.

In both cases, the issues you need to consider (and to make sure are covered in any contract) are as follows:

- *What is the brief?* What you want them to do, how quickly, in what manner and with what authority.

- *What is the cost?* The rates, the likely length of the assignment and any success or performance-related fees.

- *What degree of control do you want to exercise?* Reporting lines and direction from the business.

- *How do you get them out again afterwards?* Contract length and termination provision, and handover process at end of assignment.

Then there are the housekeeping elements:

- taking references
- hours of work, sickness/holiday arrangements, substitution provisions
- expenses
- authorisation of timesheets, billing and payment
- confidentiality and intellectual property
- liability and insurance.

MANAGING PEOPLE AND THE PROCESS OF CHANGE

You have now set your business objectives and you have decided what changes are needed. Is this enough? Will the changes simply happen or not? The answer is that, unless you make them happen, there will be no changes. And making them happen can be difficult because there are many barriers to overcome which tend to break down into the major categories shown in Figure 37:

Problem	Issue	Solution
Your staff don't know they have to change.	Lack information.	Communication of plan, goals and actions.
Your staff can't change.	Lack knowledge of what they need to do. Lack knowledge of how to do it. Lack resources (time, money, people, equipment) to allow them to do it.	Communication of plan, goals and actions. Training and support. Project management skills.
Your staff won't change.	Do not wish to make the changes.	Understand motivation Manage culture change.

Fig. 37. The barriers to change.

The techniques for addressing the critical areas of communication, project management and motivation are set out below, but you should remember that all these areas are inextricably linked.

Existing habits are hard to break. Making change happen requires applying effort to overcoming often deep-seated resistance to change in order to break out of existing ways of doing things and to create new, healthier habits. Creating effective change, therefore, usually entails going through the process shown in Figure 38.

Your staff might be reluctant to change for a wide variety of reasons:

- *Psychological* – uncertainty, fear, disorientation (so change needs to be as swift as possible to avoid nagging doubt, but slow enough to bring everyone with it).

- *Personal attitudes and beliefs* – 'we cannot deliberately underquote in the initial stages of an assignment (like everyone else in the industry does) to get the work as it just isn't right'.

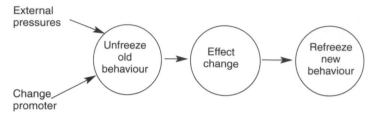

Fig. 38. The change process.

- *Group loyalty* – the sales team may fight like cats and dogs but just watch them stick together if you try to put production in charge.

- *Habit* – 'but we've always done it this way'.

- *Politics* – 'not if Joe is going to be in charge'.

- *Physiological* – the new roster of 20 consecutive night shifts is unacceptable.

To unfreeze existing behaviour, therefore, you often need the heat of external pressure (a 'burning platform') before people will realise the need to move to a new position. But you cannot simply rely on external forces to provide sufficient pressures as some of your staff will have little real immediate appreciation of your position.

You will therefore also need to *signal* major change by making your staff aware of the situation and the need for action and by making change real: by doing something that really makes people sit up and take notice.

'Barnstorming ideas' and shock tactics (and the messages they convey) can include the following:

- *Slaughtering sacred cows* – everything in your business is potentially up for radical change.

- *Killing something big* – is there a large visible project that can be axed (without threatening future development)?

- *Clearing out non-performers* – you cannot afford passengers.

- *Breaking a blocker* – if someone is actively blocking change, he or she cannot be allowed to win. Either you are with the changes and where we are going or you are against us.

Obviously, if you can get your staff to want to change (to 'buy in'), they are obviously a lot easier to manage and motivate than if you need to force them to change. Unfortunately the management style required tends to be dictated by the degree of the crisis and the speed of the response needed (Figure 39).

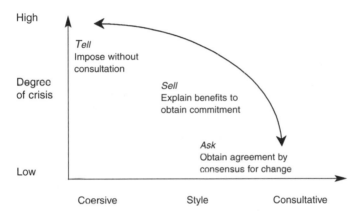

Fig. 39. Management approaches to change.

In the initial phases of a turnaround, speed of change tends to be of the essence and periods of uncertainty have to be minimised. To overcome initial confusion and lack of control as the business has got into trouble this tends to require a highly centralised and directive management style to deal with the crisis phase, which then needs to evolve into a more empowering one for the regrowth phase (Figure 40).

A compromise approach that can be very effective in empowering a team to accept a swift pace of change is the 'crisis weekend' where you get your line managers together as a group for a real crisis summit. There the team really thinks out (in a concentrated and intense atmosphere) what the situation is, what needs to happen and who is going to do what. When done

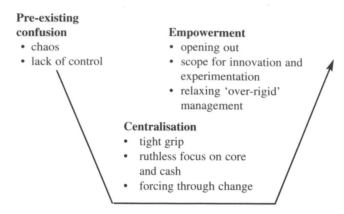

**Pre-existing
confusion**
- chaos
- lack of control

Empowerment
- opening out
- scope for innovation and experimentation
- relaxing 'over-rigid' management

Centralisation
- tight grip
- ruthless focus on core and cash
- forcing through change

Fig. 40.   Management styles to employ during a turnaround.

correctly, the team becomes a powerful committed force and never forgets 'Our twelve-hour days when we sorted out how we were going to really fix the mess'. You will need to give the team time to gel, however, as to become a team, the group has to go through the team-building process of:

1. *Storming* (arguing about how to work together).

2. *Norming* (agreeing how to work together).

3. *Performing* (acting as a team).

As you move through the process, the ways of implementing change will start with the very directing style of *fixing new habits*. For example, you might issue an instruction and check up every day for 21 days that the instruction is being followed *that day*. By the end of three weeks, however, the new way of doing something will have become the new habit. Your staff will now know that, once something has been decided, they need to do it because there is no hiding place and you will not be going away. You can then significantly relax your enforcement and policing on this particular item. This approach is, however, very time consuming and your efforts will therefore need to be clearly prioritised.

Over time you can adopt a more empowering mechanism to change your business's culture, using other management skills:

- *Walk the talk* – lead by example and get out to see and be seen.

- *Shared values* – include attitude as a basis for recruiting like-minded staff to reinforce the culture.

- *Define* what 'anti-social behaviour' (e.g. rudeness to customers, laziness) means for 'our culture'. If everyone is living the culture, the 'anti-social' can be dumped without remorse or protest.

- *Training* – the organisation's values should be specified and incorporated into training and staff development.

- *Rewards* – reward employees who act the values.

- *Value staff* – treat them like winners and care for them.

- *Celebrate success* – identify wins (especially early quick ones) and make success very visible (e.g. a bottle of champagne to people who achieve targets).

- *Celebrate creative failures* – better to try and not succeed than not to try at all, so long as the risks and downsides of failure are limited.

- *Cultivate identity* – promote your values as part of your brand. Make them real by way of uniforms, corporate colours, emblems and slogans (visit a Kwikfit for an example of this).

- *Customers first* – make the job worth while.

- *Tight culture, loose management* – give staff discretion but within the bounds of a firm set of corporate values.

When managing your staff it is important to recognise that people will have a variety of personality types and will be motivated by, and will fear, different things. You as an entrepreneur may be driven by success (and fear failure). Some of your staff may seek praise and recognition and fear rejection. Both you and these types of employees may often be quick to take decisions and may be restless, active and open for change (the 'square pegs'). Most of your staff, however, will value security and structured policies within which to work ('so they know where they stand') and will fear change, uncertainty or conflict (the 'round pegs').

You therefore need in normal times to be careful to manage your staff in a way that is appropriate to *them*. Your production staff may tend to be round pegs in the round holes of structured work and be managed in a round-peg way (e.g. with detailed instructions on how to do their particular jobs). Your sales staff, however, may tend to be square pegs in square holes who need to be managed in a square-peg way (e.g. with clear targets of sales to achieve and lots of praise for success).

This also means you need to manage the way you go about changing things to match the needs of your staff (see Figure 41). Particularly with 'round staff', managing change is about building confidence in their ability to change, and this is helped by:

- providing them with support through training and information; and

- building their trust through two-way communication, avoidance of criticisms of the past, allowing for failures and appreciating that success may take time.

Your characteristics	Your drive/ pace of change	Square staff	Round staff
Square	Fast	You will move at a speed they feel comfortable with	Your rush to change things will frighten these staff. You (and your other staff) will need to slow the pace of change and provide more support so that these staff feel secure in their ability to handle change
Round	Slow	Will be frustrated by your pace. You need to speed up your pace of change to keep them with you	You will move at a pace they feel comfortable with

Fig. 41. Adapting management style to meet the needs of staff.

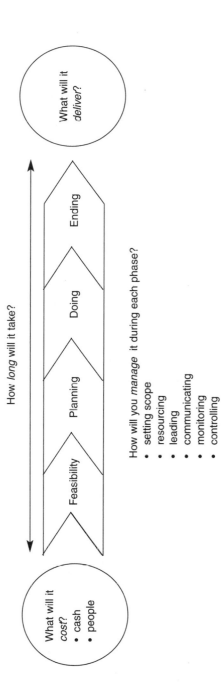

Fig. 42. Managing a project.

MANAGING A PROJECT

The things you need to know about any project – if it is to be successful – are summarised in Figure 42.

Make sure you know the answers to all these questions in respect of any project you wish to undertake.

GETTING STAKEHOLDERS ON BOARD AND KEEPING THEM THERE

There is a wide variety of people, groups and bodies who take an interest in the success of your business ('the stakeholders') and whom you might therefore wish to call on for support to see you through your difficulties and to rebuild your business.

The key stakeholders that need to be 'on board' for any turnaround are generally:

- shareholders

- directors

- management

- employees

- bankers

- trade creditors (and sometimes credit insurers, e.g. Trade Indemnity plc)

- your landlord

- customers.

- and sometimes your local authority, the Inland Revenue and/or HM Customs and Excise.

Techniques for getting each group on board and the degree of active involvement will vary, but you should prepare a brief presentation for the bank that you could also show to other stakeholders. This presentation should include the following:

- A brief high-level analysis of the business (the causes of decline, your competitive position, the key issues and your success factors).

- Your turnaround strategy.

- A copy of your action plan and forecasts.

- Details of any specific support you are seeking from them.

- Your proposals for keeping them informed of progress.

As far as possible you want a clear statement from each key stakeholder that they will support your business and that also clearly sets out any conditions they attach to that support and any reporting requirements you will need to build in to your action plan.

Ask yourself:

- How much do they stand to lose if my business fails?

- How much do they stand to gain if my business succeeds and continues to trade with them in the future? (What is in it for them?)

In general terms, the factors that will determine the degree of support you can hope to obtain from each stakeholder are exactly the same as those set out in Chapter 5 for banks.

Your communication with stakeholders needs to be full and frank and, as your plan progresses, you must keep the stakeholders informed of good and bad news in order to maintain your credibility. If you need to change your plan you will need to brief stakeholders on the change and the reason for it and to reaffirm their commitment to your plan. Ensuring that early targets are set so that they can be definitely hit will help to ensure that your credibility with stakeholders is established right from the start.

ASSESSING HOW WELL YOUR PROJECT TEAM OPERATES

Put a tick in the appropriate column for each of the statements set out overleaf, then score the test as shown.

	Disagree strongly	Disagree	Neutral	Agree	Agree strongly
Objectives					
We all know what we are trying to do					
We have realistic goals					
We know how our performance will be measured					
Approach					
We use the skills and experience of all the team					
We have open and intricate discussions					
We are flexible in how we deal with problems					
Skills and resources					
We have all the specialist skills needed					
We are all involved in decisions					
We have enough people					
We mix together easily and well					
Total ticks					
Score for each tick	–2	–1	0	1	2
Total score for each column					
Total score					

Judge your results

–20 – 5   This group is not operating as a team. What must happen to enable it to do so?

6 – 15   You are operating as a team. Which areas can you improve on?

16 – 20   You are operating so well as a team that you should be careful to avoid 'group think'.

11

Managing the Risks

IDENTIFYING THE RISKS

During a turnaround you will continue to have all your normal
responsibilities in respect of your business concerning, for
example, health and safety and environmental legislation, as
well as for keeping accounts and tax records (and, for directors,
your statutory responsibilities under the Company's Act for
filing accounts and completing an annual return).

For a business in difficulty, some of the normal business
responsibilities and risks can become particularly acute, and a
particular area to be aware of is employment law as, in turning
your business around, you will undoubtedly need to make
changes that relate to people, how they do things, who does
what and even who will still be working for you at the end of
the process.

However, employment law provides employees with
significant ranges of rights that can be enforced through
employment tribunals, potentially at significant cost to your
business. You need to be aware of these and you will need to
manage the process of dealing with employees carefully.

When dealing with a business in difficulty, however, there are
two particular areas of risk to be aware of and to manage:

1. *The personal impact on you* of dealing with the situation.

2. *Specific 'insolvency' related risks.*

DEALING WITH THE STRAIN

The sorts of basic fears we all have in varying degrees have
already been touched on, and these clearly become important in
a business in difficulty (see Figure 43).

If I fear	In a crisis, I can feel
Failure	I've failed because the business is in this mess
Rejection	My customers aren't buying or are ungrateful because they don't love me and my products any more
Instability and uncertainty	I am worrying all the time whether we are going to make it through or not
Conflict	I am having to fight the bank and say no to creditors all the time

Fig. 43. The fears involved in running a business in difficulty.

The fact is that, unless you absolutely thrive on seemingly impossible challenges (the blacker the better), having your business get into difficulty is going to be a stressful, depressing, frightening and difficult experience that is going to put a strain on you, your family and your employees.

You need to recognise these as valid, appropriate reactions and emotions. (If you did not get upset about the fact that your business is in difficulty, what does that say about you and your commitment to it?) But in recognising this you must also prevent these feelings from overwhelming you and preventing you from taking action, and you must preserve your own mental health.

You are the most important resource when it comes to restoring your business to health. If you don't do it, no one else will do it for you. The surest way to guarantee your business will fail is for you to give up trying to save it because it is 'all too difficult', 'there is nothing I can do' or 'I just can't cope'. If you are feeling depressed or stressed, see your doctor to obtain professional help to get you through this period.

INSOLVENCY-SPECIFIC RISKS

The key risks directors should be aware of in the event of a company failure are summarised in Figure 44.

For most of these risks, directors must be taken to include not only formally appointed directors but also shadow directors (people on whose instruction and direction the directors have been accustomed to act).

Person	Action	Application to partnerships/ individuals
Insolvency practitioner (IP)	Can act to set aside transactions made before the liquidation in order to increase the assets in the pot available to all creditors, such as: • **preferences** (you paid what was owed to Joe, your brother, but didn't pay any of the other creditors); and • **transactions at undervalue** (you sold Joe the company Rolls-Royce for £10 the day before the liquidation)	Similar rules apply
	Can act to make the directors personally liable to contributing towards the company's debts if he or she can prove: • **wrongful trading** (continuing to trade past the point where you knew, or ought to have known, that an insolvent liquidation was inevitable) • **fraudulent trading** (trading in a way designed to defraud creditors).	Sole traders and partners are personally liable for all the debts in a bankruptcy
DTI	Receives a report on the directors' conduct from the IP and can take action under the Company Director Disqualification Act to bar individuals from becoming company directors. In taking action they will take into account the degree of responsibility for the failure, the amount of 'Crown money' (PAYE, NI and VAT) kept by the business, the adequacy of the books and records, and statutory filing, etc.	Bankrupts are automatically barred from holding directorships during their bankruptcy
Creditors	Can seek to recover money from anyone who has given a personal guarantee ('PG') in respect of a company debt (e.g. the company leased the photocopier but you personally guaranteed the debt).	Sole traders and partners are personally liable for all their business debts in bankruptcy

Fig. 44. Risks directors face in the event of a company failure.

The following are the basic steps you should take to protect yourself from any insolvency-related action. You should make sure you are able to show that you took the appropriate steps:

- in the light of your knowledge at the time; and

- to ensure that your knowledge was as good as it could be.

You do so by demonstrating that you have:

- *Prepared and maintained accounts, trading results and forecasts.*

- If in any doubt, *taken professional advice* about whether you should continue to trade, and about any major proposed transaction (e.g. refinancing or selling major assets). For referral to an appropriate local advisor try www.turnaroundhelp.co.uk.

- *Held and minuted board meetings to record decisions and the basis on which they were made* (i.e. the forecast and professional advice received).

Remember to keep copies of all such documents.

12

Summary and Conclusion

As Robert Townsend put it in his book, *Up the Organisation*, 'If you aren't in business for fun and profit, what are you doing here?' So if it is not fun and profitable, the key steps to take are, in summary, as follows.

RECOGNISE THE NEED FOR A TURNAROUND

Spot the warning signs as early as possible. Failure is a wasting disease: the longer it is left before treatment, the weaker you are and the more radical the surgery needed. The best corporate health tip of all is to stay healthy.

STABILISE YOUR FINANCES

If you do get into difficulty, have a short-term survival plan:

* Get on top of your cash.

* Get on top of your numbers.

* Work out if you are insolvent.

* Take professional advice (www.turnaroundhelp.co.uk).

* What can you do (that is, what is in your control) to improve your profit/cash position? Don't rely on changes in what you do not totally control.

* Get credit/bank support by making yourself supportable.

DECIDE WHAT TO DO

Have a vision of what you want your business to be. Turn this into a real long-term recovery plan that matches your personal targets. Balance:

- short-term cash against long-term investment in competitiveness and value;

- staying focused on the key issues against ensuring all the detail is covered; and

- the pace at which all aspects of your business can move forwards.

Remember the formula for success (see Chapter 8):

$$A = \frac{(B, C, D) \times W^{K} - X}{£N} \; \textcircled{c}^{\text{TM}}$$

Build your business and selling effort around this and your personal objectives, and continuously refresh the formula.

MAKE IT HAPPEN

You can't rely on the turnaround fairy to make everything turn out all right. You are going to have to get out there and do it yourself. Therefore make the best use of your scarcest resource – you, your time and your enthusiasm. If you want to change people and how they do things, understand what motivates them, what will motivate them to take the action you want, and understand that what you are trying to do is to break old habits and develop new ones. Realise when you need specialist help, and get it.

Manage, manage, manage. Communicate, communicate, communicate. Never, never, never give up.

Remember to make money and to check the cash, costings and profit regularly. Be forward looking with your numbers.

Understand that change will be a continuous process, so continue to work *on* your business as well as *in* it.

CONCLUSIONS

In conclusion, therefore, I would like to wish you good luck. There is nothing so brave and demanding, or as exciting and fulfilling, as running your own business (I know) and I wish you every success.

Unfortunately I cannot hope to provide you with all the answers for your specific business. I do hope I have been able to help by providing you with the questions you can answer to give you your unique solution proposition.

Please contact me with any feedback or comments on this book, which will be gratefully received, or if you would like to discuss any aspect of the topics covered: mrblayney@aol.com; tel.: 01388 528913.

Further Information

Web-based sources of information grow daily. Here is a list of useful sites that may be of help.

RECOGNISE THE NEED FOR A TURNAROUND

www.turnaroundhelp.co.uk

Information turnaround site with access to online health checks, turnaround advice, access to services such as psychometric testing and referral service to local advisors.

www.icc.co.uk

Business data including your (and your competitors') results.

www.companywatch.co.uk

Unfortunately this site does not (yet) offer a bureau/individual report service, but it gives you an idea of the power of the financial analytical software available using H score techniques.

STABILISE YOUR FINANCES

www.turnaroundfinance.com

Portal identifying investors and lenders who claim to have a specific interest in providing finance for turnaround.

www.bba.org.uk/business

British Banking Association website. Has a glossary of banking terms and can provide details of BBA's guidelines for banks on dealing with small businesses.

www.creativefinance.co.uk

Provides small and medium-sized companies with the tools (e.g. interactive security cover calculations) and information on banks to help them deal better with their bankers as well as providing access to alternative sources of finance.

DEVISE A PLAN

www.tomedge.co.uk

Very practical tips on sales and marketing strategy and self-motivation.

www.patent.gov.uk

UK patent office. Source of information on patents, copyright, designs and trademarks.

www.reinventyourbusiness.co.uk

Small and medium-sized company business strategy consultancy.

www.internet-sales.com/hot

Collection of articles on e-business/e-markets.

www.buyabiz.com

Free access to a list of UK businesses for sale.

www.equitymatch.co.uk

Matching service for businesses with individuals seeking investment opportunities.

MAKE IT HAPPEN

www.business-toolkit.com

Cost-effective access to a database of interim managers and freelance specialist consultants.

www.r3.org.uk

Association of business recovery professionals with details of IPs, information on insolvency terms and useful links.

www.lawsociety.org.uk

Details of UK lawyers.

www.netdoctor.co.uk

Online version of Goldberg's depression test.

www.turnaround.org

Turnaround Management Association website. UK branch of an American organisation for a wide range of professionals interested in the area of turnaround and providing turnaround related services. Very wide-ranging list of links.

GENERAL SOURCES

www.managementlearning.com

Collection of free articles and training materials for managers covering most aspects of business.

www.dti.gov.uk/support

Access to the DTI's business support agencies, such as the small business service and local Business Links.

www.fsb.org.uk

Federation of Small Businesses.

www.dis.strath.ac.uk/business

General business information site.
www.howtobooks.co.uk

This book covers a wide range of areas at a general level. Find more detailed information on many of the subjects covered in other books in the range.

OTHER

In addition, most banks produce a range of leaflets and guides for small business customers, covering a variety of business sectors and issues, and many of which are available free. Contact your bank for a list.

Keep a file of good ideas and record 'best practices' when you come across them for future reference.

Read widely, not only business books (e.g. Sir John Harvey-Jones' books) but also business-orientated newspapers (e.g. *The Economist*) and your own trade press. Set yourself a target of how many business improvement ideas you will pick up a year from these sources.

Index